RACHEL MARKS 9.07

Bottom Set Citizen

While research evidence shows the negative impact of ability grouping on children, this book suggests that the reason the practice is still embraced is the unspoken allegiance to the values of empire that governments, schools, and many parents still uphold, promoting competition and hierarchies over and above ethical principles on the education of society's most vulnerable, our children.

The practice, which happens across social class, humiliates children deemed 'less academically able' by 'rounding them up' in front and in opposition to their 'better' intellectual peers. Wielding knowledge as a weapon of humiliation warps children's relationship to organized forms of knowledge, making them antagonistic or indifferent towards it. This book responds to Michael Young's *The Rise of the Meritocracy*, by focusing on the plight of those who are educationally placed in opposition to the 'intellectual elites': the bottom set citizen, rich or poor and ready to vote.

This book will appeal to anyone concerned with democracy and children's rights in education, including the rich, on whom I shine the light of deficit for a change. Thus, Donald Trump and Nigel Farage exemplify the bottom set citizen in all his facilitated glory. Other, more vulnerable BSCs are not as lucky.

Paula Ambrossi is a lecturer at the Institute of Education, University College London. Her experience as a Modern Foreign Languages teacher in secondary education, followed by almost 20 years as tutor and researcher in Primary Teacher Education, has allowed her to reflect and write on topics related to pedagogy and philosophy of education. Her recent work includes Language and Culture in Foreign Language Teaching, in *Exploring Education and Childhood: From Current Certainties to New Visions* (2015), *Mastering Primary Languages (Mastering Primary Teaching)* by Paula Ambrossi and Darnelle Constant-Shepherd (2018), *Sustaining Hegemony: Educational Use of Photographs Representing Human Distress* (2019), and *The Languages We Teach and the Empires We Embrace: Addressing Decolonization Through the Gaze of the Empire* (2024).

Routledge Advances in Sociology

381 **Globalisation and Pandemic Management**
Issues and Outcomes from COVID-19
Chris L. Peterson

382 **Education Strategy in a Changing Society**
Personalised, Smarter, Lifelong Learning in the 21st Century
Martin Slattery

383 **Magic, Science and Society**
Alex Dennis

384 **Visibilities and Invisibilities of Race and Racism**
Toward a New Global Dialogue
Yasuko Takezawa, Faye V. Harrison, and Akio Tanabe

385 **A Sociological Approach to Commodification**
The Case of Transforming the Post-Socialist Society in Poland
Marek Ziółkowski, Rafał Drozdowski and Mariusz Baranowski

386 **Bottom Set Citizen**
Ability Grouping in Schools – Meritocracy's Undeserving
Paula Ambrossi

387 **Radical Ecology in the Face of the Anthropocene Extinction**
John A. Smith and Anna Wilson

For more information about this series, please visit: www.routledge.com/Routledge-Advances-in-Sociology/book-series/SE0511

Bottom Set Citizen

Ability Grouping in Schools –
Meritocracy's Undeserving

Paula Ambrossi

LONDON AND NEW YORK

First published 2024
by Routledge
4 Park Square, Milton Park, Abingdon, Oxon OX14 4RN

and by Routledge
605 Third Avenue, New York, NY 10158

Routledge is an imprint of the Taylor & Francis Group, an informa business

© 2024 Paula Ambrossi

The right of Paula Ambrossi to be identified as author of this work has been asserted in accordance with sections 77 and 78 of the Copyright, Designs and Patents Act 1988.

All rights reserved. No part of this book may be reprinted or reproduced or utilised in any form or by any electronic, mechanical, or other means, now known or hereafter invented, including photocopying and recording, or in any information storage or retrieval system, without permission in writing from the publishers.

Trademark notice: Product or corporate names may be trademarks or registered trademarks, and are used only for identification and explanation without intent to infringe.

British Library Cataloguing-in-Publication Data
A catalogue record for this book is available from the British Library

ISBN: 978-1-032-50364-6 (hbk)
ISBN: 978-1-032-50368-4 (pbk)
ISBN: 978-1-003-39820-2 (ebk)

DOI: 10.4324/9781003398202

Typeset in Times New Roman
by Newgen Publishing UK

To my son Conrad, my sister Milena, and my friend Bruce Wilson

Contents

Lists of figures   *viii*
Acknowledgements   *ix*
List of abbreviations   *x*

Introduction   1

1 You have never been to this place   8

2 There is no democracy in childhood   32

3 Meritocracy and its allegiance to the empire   46

4 Knowledge and humiliation in schools   63

5 When knowledge does not pay   78

6 The rise of the bottom set citizen   96

7 'It never did me any harm': Some BSC exemplars   111

Index   *135*

Figures

1.1 Example of ability grouping practices in four countries 9
1.2 General structure of ability grouping within closed doors, in the United Kingdom 11
5.1 Three different colour ties to reflect three different abilities 79
5.2 Intellectual Virtues Academy (website), California 91

Acknowledgements

I would like to acknowledge all the children whose plight made me write with force and determination. I would also like to thank the following colleagues and friends who contributed in different ways, somewhere along this book-writing journey, making it a richer and less solitary one.

Priscilla Alderson, Anne Chowne, Adela Contreras, Anna Ferris, Ruth Heilbronn, Neil Selwyn, Judith Suissa, Shone Surendran, John Vorhaus, Dora Webb, and Tessa Willy.

Abbreviations

BSC   bottom set citizen
FBV   fundamental British values
ZPD   zone of proximal development

Introduction

I first walked into a UK Primary school for an observation period in September 2001, just before starting a teacher education programme. I saw that the class of 9-year-olds was grouped into four tables: the Lions, the Panthers, the Bears, and the Tigers. It was a bright, colourful, energized space, and everyone seemed happy. At one point the teacher said to me,

> Can you help the Lion's table please? They just need to fill in the gaps. You know, they're my lows.

Not being acquainted with the British educational system, I had to ask what she meant by 'lows'. She looked at me in a matter-of-fact kind of way and told me that they were her 'low ability' children. It was a moment that has stayed with me forever; I had never encountered such blasé attitude towards what I considered to be, if not an immoral, at least a highly unethical act.

Later that year, during my placement, I met Tom, a 12-year-old boy who was in my French *bottom set* class together with ten other boys and two girls.

'We're the dumb ones, Miss. That's what all the kids in school call us', he said to me with naïve sarcasm during an interview. I had arranged to talk to the 'bottom sets' for my university project, and they had been extremely keen to articulate their plight. Tom's was a challenging class due to the children's diverse needs, perceived lack of interest in languages, generally challenging behaviour, but most of all, as I came to understand, a system unable to model 'good' human interactions; where one's worth and treatment in school is not

DOI: 10.4324/9781003398202-1

dependent on one's perceived academic aptitude. I struggled with Tom's class. 'Give them no quarter' their teacher said to me at the beginning. Apparently, they were not behaving well enough for me. I was being too lenient.

In my final school placement, two university representatives came to talk to our 15-year-olds about the benefits of a degree in languages. The Head of Department did not ask the bottom set to attend because, as he explained, there was no point in it. I was left stupefied once again by his reasoning, but as a trainee teacher (and a foreigner in Britain), I did not challenge his decision or attitude.

It seems to me now that 'knowing one's place' in British society, trickles down from The Crown to the classroom, as part of a norm. Sayings like, 'better to be the tail of a lion than the head of a rat' which I had often understood as 'better to be a small part of something significant than be the protagonist of something small', suddenly revealed a darker meaning. I came across a blog post recently that held the opposite view. Dr Kenny's post quoted her father's wisdom,

> A head is a head, regardless of its size, shape, colour and pedigree. Wherever/whenever heads are called, a tail cannot present itself even if it's that of a lion.
>
> (Kenny, 2016)

Why lions should be happy to confer with their own tails when only heads are called for, is indicative of their self-importance. The rats may laugh at the contempt of the lion's tail, but such tail *claims* a stature rats can never aspire to. It seems rather silly that a mediocre tail should look down on a clever rat, but there is something interesting happening here. For instance, it was in Britain where I first heard things like, 'Nobody likes a smart Alec'. Some of my students who had done well in tests, would often ask me not to tell others. At the time I could not make sense of this request. When I was in school in Chile the opposite was the case, people encouraged and celebrated theirs and others' academic achievements. I recall taking an evening English GCSE course with a dozen other young adults when I first arrived in England. I was always putting my hand up to answer the teacher's questions. I truly believed that this was an ordinary attitude, until at one point, Sir said, somewhat irritated and without looking at me, 'Yes, yes. We know you know'. I felt terrible. When he asked other questions and no one put their hand up, neither did I. I never went back.

I later discovered that in Britain 'knowledge' is not a straightforward educational acumen. Much is tied to it that I was unaware of at the time. The meritocratic practices I had been brought up to trust obscured any insights I could have gained; for I was putting in the effort, I was doing reasonably well, participating in the best way I knew, so being shut down in that manner could only mean one of two things: either the teacher did not like me or I was doing something wrong (or being the wrong sort). I have a better idea now of what may have prompted that young teacher to say/do something like that; anything from personal circumstances to his own academic woes. Maybe he resented being 'the head of a rat', or a big fish in a little pond (Marsh et al., 2008).

Experiencing another country's educational system, as an adult, can make us reflect on things we may never have done otherwise. It can give us perspectives we never knew existed. When I mentioned ability grouping practices to some teachers in Chile, I did not expect them to exclaim, 'Gosh, that must be so difficult'. At the time I thought they meant that teaching mixed-ability classes (the only thing they knew) was easier than the thought of having to teach ability-grouped classes. But on reflection I think they meant that the process of deciding who is to go into which group would be an ethical nightmare. How do you tell the parents of 'lower ability' children? How would you tell the children? How do the children tell their parents? In most countries such a practice would be highly questionable. While meritocratic practices that group by ability *across* schools (usually into secondary education) are common worldwide (not unquestionably so), I know that Chilean parents would not tolerate their children being placed in ability groups within closed doors (in class or within school). A few did, however, have to tolerate their child repeating the academic year due to low grades, a practice that has gone out of favour these days.

A colleague recently asked me:

> What are the (historical, political) reasons why setting by ability has not been adopted in places like Chile and Finland? Is this part of an explicit political ideology? I know Finland is a very egalitarian society; but there are also surely other social and historical factors behind these differences.

This book does not go into the reasons why this may be so. However, most South American colonies were inspired in their fight for

4 Introduction

independence from the Spanish and the Portuguese, in part by the (non-native) American war of independence (1765), but in particular by the French Revolution (1789). Ideals of *freedom*, *equality* and *fraternity* seemed to dominate the spirit of independence and liberation to some extent. A similar spirit may have prevailed in Finland's ultimate independence (1917) from Sweden and Russia.

I do not mean to suggest here that there are no social injustices in other countries. There are plenty of them. However, consistently segregating pupils in front of their peers according to ability is seldom one of them. As I argue in this book, this kind of injustice does not promote epistemic virtues (e.g. appreciation for truth and knowledge and the complexities involved). On the contrary, it leaves democracy vulnerable to the impulses and reactions of a poorly informed citizenry.

It has taken me 20 years to write this book, the first 15 of which were practical in nature; in the classroom and as a lecturer. It was only when I became acquainted with Miranda Fricker's concept of epistemic injustice that I was able to fully account for my Bottom Set Citizen and for our share of the responsibility. Aspects of Critical Realism (Roy Bhaskar) allowed me to see and appreciate the many aspects that make up our educational experience. In our attempt to understand children, being adults always makes us outsiders, and it is all too easy to draw artificial lines that detach children's understanding from their day-to-day, direct experiences, thus reducing 'the potential of childhood studies to promote social justice' (Alderson, 2016: 203).

Personal experience has taken different forms in academic research and enquiry. The use of personal narrative as an enquiry method has been extensively used in social and educational research (Atkinson, 2010; Allbon, 2012; Goodson et al., 2016; Dhungana, 2022). Heuristics, whereby personal experience is itself a method of enquiry has been central to me in some important ways, instantiated not as the child experiencing 'low ability' relegation but as their teacher, and more importantly, as a citizen. It is in this last realm that I came to appreciate the greatest impact of ability grouping practices on children. For it is through the experience of being in school rather than the formal learning of facts, that we start to place ourselves as potential citizens. As Dewey said,

> To "learn from experience" is to make a backward and forward connection between what we do to things and what we enjoy or

suffer from things in consequence. Under such conditions, doing becomes a trying; an experiment with the world to find out what it is like; the undergoing becomes instruction—discovery of the connection of things.

(Dewey et al., 2002:164)

As such, how we construct the experience of being in the low or bottom set does not end when we leave school. Each reflection on the experience, thereafter, shapes the experience itself.

Consequently, this book brings together different fields of study (history, philosophy, sociology) in an effort to account for the messiness of human experience, in this instance, that of ability grouping practices within class/school.

I exemplify such practices by making reference to the United Kingdom, Australia, and the United States contexts mostly, as issues of class and race are prevalent in all three countries. It is in fact these considerations that will allow readers across many other countries to recognize similar practices employed in their own educational systems, and perhaps to reflect on the legacy of the British empire on education.

Ultimately, regardless of the way education systems operate in any given country, citizens are able to remember if and how they were grouped by academic ability while in school. Readers may recognize immediately which type of schools they attended. Teachers, parents, and those involved in educational policies will know if they support ability grouping or not. What this book is concerned with is the notion that being intellectually labelled as 'low ability' throughout one's childhood—by any other name—hurts society just as much as any other mass injustices.

In Chapter 1, I introduce the context from which as an educator I speak, and on which as a researcher I reflect. I describe what ability grouping practices are, and how they are enacted in slightly different ways across the handful of powerful countries that embrace them. I look at what the research shows in terms of the academic inefficacy of ability grouping practices for children placed in 'low ability' groups or classes, regardless of social class.

In Chapter 2, I claim that grouping children by ability can only be the product of an autocratic system that dismisses some of the basic rights of the children placed in bottom sets, i.e. to fulfil their full potential, and to have the best interests of the child as a primary consideration.

I suggest that we need to examine our own understanding of what it means to do something 'for the child's own good', as well as needing to remember the vulnerability of childhood.

In Chapter 3, I focus on how current notions of empire, rather than neo-liberalism, support the blatant meritocratic segregation practices that take place in classrooms and schools, making ability grouping appear as common-sense because of unspecified 'traditional values'. I discuss how imperial values mingle with meritocratic practices and give rise to new kinds of hierarchies and divisions in society, just as Michael Young predicted (1994). I further argue that in the educational context these hierarchies and divisions widen the breach between those who 'know' and those who do not, to everyone's detriment.

In Chapter 4, I discuss the work of Miranda Fricker related to epistemic injustice, arguing that 'low ability' grouping constitutes a *structural testimonial and hermeneutic injustice*. This implicates respectively, educational systems, what a child can declare as 'what he or she knows', and the child's inability to successfully articulate the injustice inflicted. I argue that the 'assessment of knowledge' is thus used as a means to humiliation at the hands of the persons in charge of the child's very well-being, leaving the child vulnerable to the contempt of their peers. All of this, in pursuit of an academic achievement engineered never to materialize (Francis et al., 2019).

In Chapter 5, I discuss how, by turning their back on knowledge, children learn to survive the humiliation of being placed in 'low ability' groups. I use some of the work by Lev Vygotsky (1978) 'zone of proximal development' which provides a theoretical framework to explore what happens in 'low ability' groups in terms of the 'most knowledgeable other' (Abtahi et al., 2017). I also make further reference, while exploring classroom interactions, to Hannah Arendt's (1958) ideas on *action*, and how we disclose ourselves as individuals in unintentional ways.

In Chapter 6, I give the fullest account of the Bottom Set Citizen, a concept I developed in response to Michael Young's original dystopian idea of meritocracy, as well as an outcome of our inattention to what being a citizen constitutes within John Dewey's understanding of democracy in education. I argue that BSCs find some solace in social media, which comes to be a sort of post-truth nation and home to the BSC, bestowing a sense of empowerment they may never have felt before.

In Chapter 7, I exemplify the concept of 'bottom set citizen' via three examples. Donald Trump from the United States and Nigel

Farage from the United Kingdom exemplify current BSCs with their particular kind of disdain for the establishment. Jay Blades (creator of the television program, The Repair Shop) on the other hand exemplifies a 'recovered' case—someone from a disadvantaged background who used to be a BSC but who, in his own words, managed to repair his life against all the odds. I urge schools not to promote Bottom Set Citizens; to stop the practice of ability grouping, and to encourage epistemic virtue in all our children, for they will become all our voters.

References

Abtahi, Y., Graven, M., & Lerman, S. (2017). Conceptualising the more knowledgeable other within a multi-directional ZPD. *Educational Studies in Mathematics*, *96*(3), 275–287.

Alderson, P. (2016). The philosophy of critical realism and childhood studies. *Global Studies of Childhood*, *6*(2), 199–210.

Allbon, C. (2012). "Down the rabbit hole"—"curiouser and curiouser": Using autoethnography as a mode of writing to re-call, re-tell and re-veal bodily embodiment as self-reflexive inquiry. *Journal of Organizational Ethnography*, *1*(1), 62–71.

Arendt, H. (1958). *The human condition; (Charles R. Walgreen Foundation Lectures)* (3rd Printing). University of Chicago Press.

Atkinson, B. (2010). Teachers responding to narrative inquiry: An approach to narrative inquiry criticism. *The Journal of Educational Research (Washington, D.C.)*, *103*(2), 91–102.

Dewey, E., Dewey, J., & Maxcy, S. J. (2002). *John Dewey and American education. Vol. 2. Schools of tomorrow.* Thoemmes.

Dhungana, S. (2022). Dialogic storying: A narrative research methodology in English language education. *Qualitative Research Journal*, *22*(2), 173–187.

Francis, B., Taylor, B., Tereshchenko, A., Taylor, B., & Tereshchenko, A. (2019). *Reassessing 'Ability' grouping: Improving practice for equity and attainment.* Routledge.

Goodson, I., Antikainen, A., Andrews, M., & Sikes, P. (2016). *The Routledge international handbook on narrative and life history.* Routledge.

Kenny, D. (2016, June 3). Would you rather be a tail of a lion or a head of a rat? Chatwithdrkenny.

Marsh, H. W., Seaton, M., Trautwein, U., Lüdtke, O., Hau, K. T., O'Mara, A. J., & Craven, R. G. (2008). The Big-Fish-Little-Pond-Effect stands up to critical scrutiny: Implications for theory, methodology, and future research. *Educational Psychology Review*, *20*(3), 319–350.

Young, M. (1994). *The rise of the meritocracy* (2nd ed.). Transaction Publishers.

1 You have never been to this place

The title of this chapter is indicative of a two-fold idea. Firstly, 'bottom set citizens' will not have been encouraged, through educational experience, to want to engage with research (or books like this one), and will not willingly seek or accept knowledge from established sources. Secondly, most children who go on to higher education ('high ability'), and therefore most persons in academia, have never been to this place (the bottom sets) on a permanent basis. They may have experienced relegation to bottom sets for a particular subject (which can be injury enough), but not continuously in both primary and secondary education for two or more subjects. The latter point is what this book mostly takes up, arguing that we (those reading this book) have never been to this place, and that we should ensure no one does.

The reason I never went to this place myself is because I grew up in Chile, where there are no sustained ability grouping practices within class or school. This does not mean that there are no educational injustices in Chile, or in most other countries where mixed-ability grouping is the norm, but rather, that such notions are not part of the teaching organization within classrooms or school. There is plenty of inequality *across* schools and across districts. Chile is one of South America's most unequal societies in this respect (Luna and Medel, 2023).

In countries like Britain, the United States, Australia, and South Africa, grouping school children by ability has a history as long as the British Empire. It could be seen as one of the legacies of empire; either in terms of introducing such practices or consolidating and augmenting already existing hierarchies (Pomfret, 2015), like cast systems in India (Chakravorty, 2019). Although enacted differently in different countries, the practice entails the grouping of children—within the *same class* or within the *same school*—according to an assessed academic ability for some subjects.

The form of segregation that this book objects to, principally, is the one that happens within closed doors (same class or same school); the one that is seldom advertised in schools' websites, and the one that can expose children to the daily contempt of their peers.

In most US high schools, children are tracked according to ability and placed in either high or low track classes. The 'bottom set', the 'low track', the 'low like-group', the 'low-attainment group', etc., are all euphemisms for the same experience: for teachers, the (unfounded) belief that grouping by ability is a harmless, academically beneficial practice for all children; but for the children in the lower sets, the experience is the humiliation of being consistently labelled as 'intellectually inferior' to their peers. Such an experience has significant implications for those children's future relationship with notions of what is worth knowing and understanding; implications that work against the grain of a democracy constituted by 'informed' citizens.

Grouping by ability in schools

Although I consider the practice of ability grouping 'within closed doors' the most academically and emotionally damaging kind for children in the 'lower ability' groups, it is by no means the only objectionable kind. The table (Figure 1.1) serves as an exemplification of the types of ability grouping practices that are most common. It is not an exhaustive list.

Age range	Some examples of most common types of ability groupings			
	Australia	United Kingdom	United States	Spain
5 to 11 year-olds	within class like-groups and between class streaming	within class ability grouping	within class ability grouping	no ability grouping
	between school ability grouping, and:			
12 to 16 or 18	between class streaming	between class setting	between class tracking	at 15, between class tracking

Figure 1.1 Example of ability grouping practices in four countries.

I have chosen Spain as the 'control' group, exemplifying the usual situation found in most other countries where there is little or no within class/school ability grouping. In France, for instance, pupils *choose* different paths at the age of 16. In Austria and Germany this happens at 12. Although many schools in the United States had stopped the practice for 5- to 11-year-olds, there has been a resurgence (Brown Center, 2013).

Scandinavian nations tend to have comprehensive systems of education with no within school ability grouping. In Finland, for instance, as Kosunen et al. observe, 'standardized testing, inspection, a detailed national curriculum, hard evaluation, competition, or accountability have not been introduced into a great extent' (Kosunen et al., 2020: 1467).

In terms of between-school ability grouping, there are of course many factors that can impact school choice or allocation, with ability being only one of them (i.e. economic status, religious beliefs, parental engagement, etc.). It is very difficult however, to separate these other factors from a child's results in an entry exam to an academically demanding school. Kosunen et al. (2020) observe that on entering secondary education in Finland, socioeconomic background shapes parent and pupil choice, which impacts the type of study group (or school) children attend. This indirect type of segregation, despite overall efforts to the contrary in many places, hides, exacerbates, and maintains social inequities, and is therefore also an objectionable practice with no easy solution.

In schools that do not group by ability (France, Spain, Chile, etc.), children may well be known for their abilities or struggles with certain subjects, and they may well suffer the daily stress of tests or parental pressure. What they will not suffer however, is the direct, daily humiliation that children within the same class or school suffer, when placed consistently in the 'lower ability' groups or tracks. It is this daily experience of being *seen* as inferior; of being *identified* as in contrast to the 'more able' peers, that makes ability grouping within class and within school, a most objectionable and unethical practice.

Setting: ability grouping in the United Kingdom

The practice of 'setting' or grouping children in classrooms and within school according to their academic ability (Figure 1.2) is a milder version of an old British tradition: streaming. Streaming involved the same rationale of grouping pupils by ability, but in much more

Figure 1.2 General structure of ability grouping within closed doors, in the United Kingdom.

rigid ways. In Britain, streaming was an explicit, expected, and accepted academic practice since 1862. However, grouping children according to their assessed intellectual ability, did not reach a national momentum until the eugenics movement was established. According to the National Human Genome Research Institute, eugenics, whose main proponent was Sir Francis Galton, is the scientifically erroneous and immoral theory of 'racial improvement' and 'planned breeding'. The Eugenics Society maintained that intelligence was inherited and that therefore, each child was born with a given intellectual capacity that remained the same over time; that could be accurately measured; that could ultimately be used to ensure the right mind got the right kind of employment and breeding opportunities (Stone, 2002; Chitty, 2009; Choudhury, 2015). Giving the right kind of education to the right kind of mind was therefore seen as the first step towards achieving this principle. The issue of selecting the best children for the best schools was part of the 1923 Eugenics Review, which sought to ensure that the best of Britain was prepared to occupy the ruling positions in society. The major issue, it was argued, was to find 'the real aristocracy of the nation' (in Chitty, 2009: 72).

These were apt words when we consider that in many ways, a new aristocracy was exactly what was achieved with the advent of the intellectual elites: an intellectual aristocracy. However, whereas one could marry, work or pay one's way into the old aristocracy, intelligence was not something that could be bought or earned in any way. The glass ceiling of intelligence appeared to be completely impenetrable; one was either born intelligent or not. Although the certification of one's intelligence through diplomas and degrees is socially and historically situated (Lowe, 2021; Martin, 2022), the piece of paper that carries such certification can be obtained through other, less rigorous processes. Degrees and diplomas have been known to be falsified or bought, betraying their desirability in an age of, as Sandel (2020) puts it, *The tyranny of merit*.

An admirer and follower of the eugenics movement was Sir Cyril Burt (1883–1971), a geneticist and educational psychologist whose main focus was the education of Britain. Burt possessed, 'a keen interest in measurement and quantification; and an anxiety to prevent the deterioration of the race by ensuring that the "able" and the "gifted" were given the positions of authority in society that their intelligence merited' (Chitty, 2009: 69). Thus, in 1944, the *eleven plus* (11+) test was designed to determine which 11-year-olds could go on to pursue an academic education at a Grammar School, and by default, which could not. The exam tested children's English and Mathematical abilities as well as their verbal and non-verbal reasoning skills. The reader can easily access sample papers from the Internet. In them one can appreciate that these exams are in fact a kind of I.Q. test (intelligence test), and many adults struggle with them today. One example (verbal reasoning) asks children to mark two words, one from each set of brackets, that complete the sentence in the most *sensible* way:

Help is to (relieve serve assist) as **hinder** is to (prevent impede defy)[*]

Only one pairing is correct, while eight are supposedly incorrect. Instructions that appeal to what we deem as 'sensible' require a great deal of inculturation already.

[*] assist/impede

Grammar schools thus, only accept children who passed their 11+ exam, but even then, children would still be placed in top, middle, or bottom sets accordingly. Those in the bottom sets might find some consolation in the proverb, 'better to be the tail of a lion than the head of a rat'.

The idea that intelligence ought to be used as a criterion for academic merit was the starting point for Michael Young's 1994 dystopian satire, The Rise of the Meritocracy, which this book responds to. Over 20 years later, his son, Toby Young, observed that his father strongly mistrusted the introduction of the 11+.

> It wasn't just the sorting of children into sheep and goats at the age of eleven that my father objected to. As a socialist, he disapproved of equality of opportunity on the grounds that it gave the appearance of fairness to the massive inequalities created by capitalism. He feared that the meritocratic principle would help to legitimise the pyramid-like structure of British society.
>
> (Young, 2015)

We will come back to this idea in Chapter 3, but it serves here to understand how the 11+ was the first, concrete, and official instantiation of ability grouping practices for children within and across schools, at a national scale. Not all parents believe in a Grammar school education today. There is still political controversy over their existence (McInerney, 2013). The practice never had, in ways we can appreciate now, any honourable beginnings, and yet, similar academically selective entry processes are still practised by many schools around the world today. Nothing new there. We have all bought into the idea that hard work merits rewards (good grades, opportunities, financial stability, professional status, etc.). The issue with academic merit however, is that its effort is tied to the idea of intellectual and individual differences. This means that it is no longer hard work that necessarily gets the best grades and opportunities. We have all heard of exceptional work as being 1% inspiration and 99% hard work. Children are constantly told about the importance of hard work. And yes, there is truth in this. But many children also learn by themselves that hard work does not always, of itself, merits rewards. Something else does, and they know it. Academic ability does not go unnoticed by children in school, particularly where adults make a point of it. What children unfortunately are not aware of is that ability itself is the product of many things in their life and not just a reflection of their identity. Socioeconomic background, parental education levels, one's own personality traits, and even luck are all implicated in our successes and failures.

The 11+ exam is no longer a blanket requirement for all children leaving primary education. Streaming and sorting children nationwide by their level of intelligence was ultimately deemed damaging for their success potential (Plowden, 1967: 292). Nowadays in Britain, anyone wanting to attend a Grammar school must pass that school's own version of the 11+. For the wealthy who fail, private schooling is an option. Most children in the United Kingdom however, go on to state secondary schools automatically. Here, a different, more covert kind of segregation takes place, and it maintains a similar ethos of giving 'the best' opportunities to the minds that merit it the most.

Schools no longer have different tier systems (streams) where entire cohorts are segregated according to ability and for all subjects. These days only certain subjects are implicated. Mathematics, the subject where ability segregation practices are most common (Fuligni et al., 1995; Boaler et al., 2000; Venkatakrishnan, 2003; Zevenbergen, 2005), is followed closely by science, English, and foreign languages (Hallam and Ireson, 2008; Kayumova and Dou, 2022). The idea is that children can interact with all classmates in other subjects, and that through effort, they can easily move up levels within their year for the ability-set subjects. In this way, secondary schools can have up to five or more ability sets per year, per subject; from the *top set* for the high attainers, to the *bottom set* for the children who struggle most.

I once taught in a school that had eight sets for Mathematics for their 12-year-olds. Who were the children in the bottom set? The answer is a rather obvious one in state schools: boys usually, refugee children, children mostly from disadvantaged backgrounds and ethnic minorities. In private schools however, the bottom sets are composed of children who have no recourse; no social injustices that might explain their plight. Ultimately, whatever the social, emotional, or psychological reasons behind their circumstances, the reason why so many children are *not* in the top sets is because they cannot achieve at the same level of other 'more able' peers. For many children, being moved from the top set to the middle set—let alone from the middle to the bottom set, is a personal and social calamity (Boaler et al., 2000; Hansen, 2008; Reay, 2017; Francis et al, 2019; Spina, 2019; Towers et al., 2019; McGillicuddy and Devine, 2020).

Tracking in the United States: nature and nurture debates

In a 2008 article critiquing ability grouping in young children, Bruce Hanson, a teacher from the United States, recalls his own young daughter's distress one day:

> I held her heaving body and cooed daddy/daughter things until she began to relax. When she finally caught her breath, all she could croak out was "I'm going to be a bluebird." I mouthed to my wife, Sharon, "What's a bluebird?" Mystified, I held my despondent daughter until she could breathe normally. It turns out Lindsey had read poorly with Mrs. Greenseth that day. Afterward, Lindsey convinced herself that she would be moved into the lower achieving reading group—the bluebirds.
>
> (Hansen, 2008, par1)

What baffled Hanson during a subsequent parents' meeting, was that Mrs Greenseth had convinced herself that the children were not aware which reading level they belonged to. Many teachers believe that the various, neutral names given to ability groups (Lions, Reds, etc.) hides their labelling purposes. Many parents too, whether in the United States, United Kingdom, Australia, etc., are not aware that their young children are being grouped by ability in the classroom. Such information is never displayed on schools' websites.

As little Lindsey's case demonstrates, the thought of being labelled as a 'lower achiever' can prey heavily on a young mind; being thus classified and identified is a social tragedy. It suggests that even children learn to associate an ability, like reading, with one's personal identity; a lifting of the veil on individual differences of worth; a spotlight on who we are as persons, as intrinsically us: 'I am a good/bad reader'. One can see how children might prefer to say that they either hate or are not interested in reading, rather than identify themselves as 'a bad reader'.

There have been some significant attempts to de-tracking the school system in the United States. During the civil rights movement in the 1960s, issues of race related to opportunity and attainment in school became a cause for concern. Subsequent research on the topic finally showed that ability grouping restricted access to knowledge to the most vulnerable groups—often placed in lower tracks (Murphy and Hallinger, 1989; Welner and Oakes, 1996), and that it caused unequal educational opportunities, encouraging students' racial and socioeconomic stratification (Burris and Garrity, 2008). The initial evidence led to further exemplifications of good practice, where a top-down approach to de-tracking in schools was advocated (Welner and Oakes, 1996). Despite subsequent positive evidence from de-tracked schools, including longitudinal data that showed the benefits of de-tracking in the United States (Burris and Garrity, 2008), the benefits of mixed-ability grouping did not seem to outweigh meritocratic and individualistic practices.

In his book, 'Dumbing down our kids: Why American children feel good about themselves but can't read, write, or add', C. J. Sykes (1994) spoke to the concern of many (particularly conservative) parents and teachers in relation to how able children were not only no longer being pushed academically, but were in fact being robbed of the opportunity to achieve what they were capable of achieving, by having to learn 'creatively' (learning through play and activities) rather than traditionally (memorizing/analysing facts). I imagine that a reversed title for his book would read something like, 'Why American children feel bad about themselves, but can at least read, write, and add'. Of course, we want a child that is both happy and able to read, write, add, etc. The issue is not about depriving the so-called 'more able' child from challenges and opportunities, but how to do so without limiting the horizons of others.

There has thus been a resurgence of ability grouping in the United States, driven partly by parents' desire to have their children pushed academically in order to access the best colleges (Ansalone, 2010; Stark, 2014), and by teachers' misguided belief that children who struggle get in the way of this aim. As an Australian secondary teacher candidly put it, some schools become, 'much better at weeding those kids out' (in Spina, 2019) than others, by which was meant 'out of academic subjects' that lead to university pathways.

Sharing the same language and similar cultural elements with the United Kingdom, the eugenics movement is also responsible for indirectly encouraging ability grouping practices in the United States. There is a huge industry of standardized intelligence tests that dominate access to education in the United States (Sacks, 1999; Knoester and Au, 2017). This is particularly relevant when we consider the links between eugenics and race in a country marked by the never-healing scars of the slave trade, the ensuing segregation practices, and the continued inequities and covert exclusions that black people suffer in a supposedly non-racist society. Thus, ability grouping in the United States is not just a matter regarding a child's ability, but also a way of maintaining white privilege for the elites (Stark, 2014). Welner (1996) called it 'racial tracking' or what is also known as 'second generation segregation', where schools treated (and many still do) immigrants coming to America as second class citizens who needed only a basic, work-oriented education. A preparation for college was reserved for those who were seen as gifted, born to or suited for such roles. It is in fact through the concept of giftedness, argues Stark (2014) that ability grouping is not truly about ability; notions of giftedness and ability have both been 'formed through key racial projects in the history of US schooling' (Stark, 2014: 395).

Grouping by ability hides ideas and values around hierarchies, power and control, not only in the United Kingdom and United States but also, for instance, in other English-speaking countries where this practice has been challenged, like Australia (Spina, 2019) and South Africa (Chisaka and Vakalisa, 2003; Hove, 2022).

The tragedy is that ability, like race, is often treated at school as bound in nature, that is to say, aspects we are born with and which cannot be nurtured as such. When schools speak of nurturing talent or ability, they mean literally to feed (through the curriculum and resources) what is already there and primed. Grouping by ability would not make sense otherwise. It is the *outcomes* of the child's talents and abilities that schools feel they can improve, not the ability itself. And here's the rub, for it is on the assessment of those very outcomes that ability itself is afterwards labelled. Such circularity keeps things as they are. Those children in the low track, like those in the bottom set, seldom move up to a higher ability level (Francis et al., 2019). Under the banner of American choice and personalized learning, grouping by ability appears to be a legitimate and desirable practice, as if education were a marketable, tailored product that can suit everyone's needs as long as those needs are identified. In their highly acclaimed book, *The buying and selling of American education*, Zelman and Sorensen (2022) make a well-sustained, but ultimately meritocratic and capitalist case for making schools more accountable for the success of every child. Their suggestions, which include moving funding from schools to the students themselves, are radical but still within a frame of buyers' choice (this time the community itself) and meritocratic practices which sees children as either deserving or undeserving of academic success according to test results or parental choice of school. In the latter case, parents in the United States seem to have bought into the idea of ability grouping, particularly when it comes to high achieving children. Parents support the tracking system as the fairest way for their children to succeed (Ansalone, 2010), but they seldom imagine that their child will be placed in the low track. The issue remains however, that most of the success falls to the privileged children, regardless of race (Lareau, 2011), showing simply that such children are better trained at navigating a privileged and often white system.

What the research says

If the evidence in the past 20 years shows anything consistently, is that ability setting has a detrimental effect on many children as well as inflicting humiliation for those in the 'low ability' groups or sets (Chisaka and Vakalisa, 2003; Burris and Garrity, 2008; Archer et al., 2018; Towers et al., 2019; McGillicuddy & Devine, 2020). Neither does ability grouping have particular benefits on most children (Tomlinson, 1999; Barnett and Lamy, 2013; Tienken and Zhao, 2013). We should therefore ask ourselves why schools continue with this practice. What sort of 'good' does it serve? I ponder more deeply on what is meant by the 'good' of something in Chapter 2, but I mention it here because I want to look at research that attempts to explain teachers' common-held beliefs about ability grouping and its possible reasons; as well as on children's own views on the matter.

Some research, for example, shows that ability grouping is a response to parents wanting their 'talented' children to receive the best opportunities a school can offer, in a classroom that nurtures and challenges them academically (Ansalone, 2010; Carter and Welner, 2013). I do not believe many would argue with this. We all may want the same for our children, *whatever* their perceived ability, which is why most other countries do not see the need to group by ability, for all children can be made to feel differently challenged by similar content, and many differences in mixed-ability settings are due to social orientations and gender related considerations than purely to attainment itself (Silvers, 2009; Hove, 2022).

Other research points to logistics as a reason for grouping by ability, i.e. ease of planning and delivery, or 'the practicalities in the classroom' (Towers et al., 2019: 31). Such reasons are usually centred on the teacher rather than the learner.

Teaching bottom sets, with their usual behaviour management demands, can be a highly stressful environment for teachers (Klassen, 2010; Collie and Mansfield, 2022), and some research mentions the strategies teachers use to counter the situation. Teachers saying things like,

> it's not fair to give somebody [a teacher] all the higher ability ones, and none of the lower ability ones. And, it would be unfair to give somebody all the lower ability ones, especially if you had a bottom set.
> (Francis et al., 2019: 125)

The rewards of working with bottom sets are personal and not immediate, and can have a high emotional cost. Although children from top sets may learn quickly, one gets the feeling that they will succeed with or without you, to greater or lesser extents. On the other hand, when working with children who struggle, you have to be on your toes, and equipped with a range of methodological approaches that can motivate them at a personal level, which is not easy when they feel already labelled as 'low ability'. Such children may present the greatest pedagogical challenge but can also confer a greater sense of professional satisfaction.

Some research made sense of ability grouping as a, 'practice of division' that 'classifies', 'distributes', and 'excludes' groups, a 'system which regularly sorts children on the basis of their usefulness within the testing regime, or their perceived "gaps" in learning' (Bradbury et al., 2021: 158).

This high-stakes accountability climate, based on performativity in the form of standards, targets, and league tables, can turn teachers into what Wilkins (2011) called, a 'post-performative' actor: teachers themselves having been brought up within a performative system.

One of my student teachers once said, as a response to a discussion on ability grouping, that children ought to get used to this practice because it was 'the way of the world'. Having spent her whole life in the UK educational system, she had internalized the practice as an expected, unquestioned event (which probably worked in her favour). As such, she is likely to sustain the practice despite what the research shows. Take, for example, what this teacher says,

> I have read the research that says setting doesn't work and it shouldn't be happening. I've read all of that and I understand the logic behind it but the practicality in the classroom is the demands on me to get through that Year 5 curriculum [9-year-olds].
>
> (in Towers et al., 2019: 31)

This 'practicality in the classroom' which appeals to common-sense would seem to be holding performativity and the demands for accountability responsible for the continuation of ability grouping practices. I am not entirely convinced by this reasoning any more than I would hold hunger and a restaurant menu responsible for unhealthy eating (although they may be implicated). There are many ways of being held to account. Accountability and performativity do not depend on ability grouping for their exercise. They are rather, aspects that impact teaching and learning in ways I cannot go into here. Many countries that do not group children by ability in school, still have to account for their progress, mostly in summative ways like tests and exams, a dubious practice in itself that has not been thus far seriously challenged (Rees, 2013). Yes, it can be disheartening to always get the lowest grades, but at least it is not as humiliating as being put in a separate table or class on account of it. Differentiation by outcome, where all students receive the same input which each child meets differently, is a good compromise in mixed-ability settings. Effective mixed ability teaching however, requires a highly pedagogically resourceful teacher (Dudley, 2015).

Ultimately, research shows that the academic gains that ability grouping may have for the few children in the top sets (Preckel et al., 2019) does not excuse the academic, social, and emotional harm done to many children in the bottom sets:

> setting reflects and illuminates inequitable social and educational trends. [it] could be viewed as an educational technology that both reflects and reproduces the interests of dominant social groups, by reproducing relations of privilege [including] … the classed nature of 'ability' (the concentration of middle-class pupils in top sets and working-class pupils in lower sets); and the cultural dominance of 'whiteness' (White pupils being more likely to be directed to top sets, Black pupils to low sets). … with working-class pupils being most affected by school messages about their 'ability' identity (Abraham, 1995; Hamilton, 2002).
>
> (in Francis et al., 2019: 72)

One of the valuable aspects in many of the studies mentioned so far is the child's voice that comes through; observations from school children themselves on their plight, and the plight of their peers. The excerpts below are from three separate studies, and they span over 20 years. The first one, from Boaler et al. (2000) observes how youngsters construct self-perception, stripping their language of the euphemisms used by adults (i.e. top set or high track; bottom set or low track) using instead the plain language children use to refer to each other.

> I prefer groups when we're all mixed up. There's the clever and the dumb and the dumb learn from the clever and sometimes the clever they'll be learning from the people who don't know as much.
> (in Boaler et al., 2000: 643)

In Tyson's study (2013) we hear from a school-leaver's public response, following a statement where the school Principal had praised his school's achievements in terms of inclusion of minority, black students. The school-leaver wrote:

> Statistics simply fail to address the stark separations within. Enloe enrols many minority students from various ethnic backgrounds, but in all my four years there have never been more than two Black students in any one of my classes. Often there are none.
> (in Tyson, 2013: 171)

Francis et al.'s (2019) study is reminiscent of my own school experience as a young teacher in 2001. It shows, like the previous excerpts, how aware children are of their plight in bottom sets; the embarrassment and absurdity, as well as the helplessness behind it all.

'Sauda: I feel like some people, well, a lot of people, I think everybody, they feel like, when they look at their thing and they think, 'Oh, I'm in Set 5,' they get upset. And it's embarrassing to walk into, like, a Set 5 class, or a Set 4 class.
Raad: Yeah, they tease you.
Sauba: Yeah.
Interviewer: Do they?
All: Yeah.

Interviewer: Have you seen that happen?
All: Yeah.
Interviewer: What sort of things happen?
Sauba: It's like, 'Shut up, you're dumb, you're in Set 5. I'm smarter than you,' just that, you know. And I think that can bring down people's self-esteem.
Afraima: And they just brag about what they've got, like, high marks and stuff like that, and we're just like, 'Hello?'
(in Francis et al., 2019: 77)

Children seize the opportunity to tell adults about their predicament, just like my bottom sets were eager to tell me about theirs (see Introduction). What goes through their mind when weeks, months, or years pass and nothing changes, is rather sad to contemplate. I imagine they learn that if adults know about certain injustices and they do nothing about them, it is probably okay to perpetrate them, or, more worryingly, that humiliating others on account of their academic ability is not really an injustice. Like another boy said in Frances et al.'s study, 'You just have to get used to it' (ibid: 81).

No social class is safe

Grouping by ability in schools has no class boundaries. Private schools segregate students by ability and often in much more rigid ways, in an attempt to maintain or emulate traditional ways of teaching, within a system of hierarchies, where streaming and setting were/are a norm (Charlton et al., 2007; Cowan, 2020). We have come to understand superficially how private schools, particularly boarding schools work, through such films as Tom Brown School Days (1940), Jane Ayre (1943), If (1968), David Copperfield (1935, 1970, 2019), The Prime of Miss Jean Brodie (1969), Dead Poets Society (1989), Harry Potter (2001–2011), etc. Such films often portray, together with the perceived abandonment of children by parents, a hostile school environment of competition and survival, of harshness and a lack of emotional care from peers and significant school adults. Notwithstanding all this, and perhaps to a point because of all this, they also offer the idea of power, superiority, uniqueness, and future connections, and appeal therefore to those parents who seek all or some of these characteristics for their children, and are of course in a position to pay for it. However, money will not guarantee that their child will be placed in the top set. Yes, children in the bottom set of a private school may get a much better deal than the equivalent children from state schools in terms of educational resources, personalized learning, and dedicated time from teachers, but they may also experience, like Sauda from one of the previous excerpts, the humiliation of walking into that bottom set or low track classroom; of encountering, for the first time perhaps, one of the things money cannot buy.

The point I wish to make is that being wealthy offers no protection from the humiliation of being placed in 'low ability' groups. How the child and the family cope with that humiliation however, can vary. Wealthy parents can choose from hiring after-school tutors to buying complete home-school education, or, like any parents might, play down the importance of school learning in an effort to raise or maintain theirs and their child's self-esteem. Ultimately, we all know that it is possible for the very-wealthy to buy degrees and diplomas if needed, where most if not all of the coursework is in fact done by someone else. The alleged bought degree by the prince of Qatar at UCLA (United States) (LA Times, 2020) is one example. The Varsity Blues Trial is another, where many US wealthy (and famous) parents were found guilty of paying their children's way into elite colleges and universities (Medina et al., 2019).

The wealthy will always have an advantage in terms of available options for their children. I only wish to emphasize here that the feeling of humiliation in terms of intellectual inferiority is not necessarily foreign to the wealthy or the better-off, and, as I will claim in Chapter 7, can lead to more powerful negative consequences for us all.

Likewise, coming from an intellectually strong family (the new aristocracy that the eugenics movement wished to create) does not guarantee—although it can certainly help—easy access to top sets. In Japan for instance, family and societal pressure to pass the high school entrance examinations produces great stress on children (Limura, 2018). How some children cope with the humiliation of failing to meet their parents' high expectations cannot be stated enough (Hajar, 2018), but it is difficult to regulate parental expectations and practice in the same way we can regulate schools. There is something practical we can do regarding how schools' practices impact on the stress levels of children. Having excessive parental expectations may be bad enough without adding 'ability grouping' practices at school.

The philosopher, Eva Kittay, reflects on her early reactions to having an intellectually disabled child. Although such a child may never go to an ordinary school, it shows nonetheless the parental apprehension of having a child who cannot participate in our lives in expected ways.

> We, her parents, were intellectuals. I was committed to a life of the mind … . This was the air I breathed. How was I to raise a daughter that would have no part of this? If my life took its meaning from thought, what kind of meaning would her life have?
>
> (Kittay, 2019: 5)

Fortunately for her daughter, Kittay was able to rise to the occasion, focusing instead on what truly makes us all, human beings worthy of moral parity.

There is another important difference between private and state schools in terms of how children in bottom sets are treated by teachers, and this has to do with the expectations of paying parents. Whereas in a state school teachers may be left to their own personal and professional judgements in terms of their attitude to certain children, in some private schools there may be a hidden agenda of not upsetting the parents (paying customer) by not upsetting the child; of indirectly spelling out to parents how their child will not suffer (in this private school) what may have been the norm in old-style private schools. One thing that can be guaranteed is that no allusion to existing ability grouping practices will be found on private schools' websites (or any school's website). If schools consider ability grouping practices as beneficial, should it not be clearly stated somewhere? Teachers will no doubt tell the child that he, for instance, has been placed in the bottom set for his own good. I imagine they will not tell him, let alone his parents, what the research actually suggests; that he is there for the good of others (Francis et al., 2019). I say more on private education in Chapter 7.

Why you have never been to this place

As academics, we simply do not know what it is like to suffer knowledge; to be told that what really matters in life is what we know, while at the same time being made to feel unable to 'know' in the same way as praise-worthy others. 'Trust me. I know what I'm talking about. I've been there. I was a "low ability" school child most of my time there'. Such utterances are not truly available to us. Of course, I do not need to lose a limb in order to know that such condition would change my life radically. I do not need to suffer the loss of a loved one in order to understand that loss can shutter someone's life. In the same way, I do not need to suffer segregation to know that the practice will have adverse effects on someone who lives through it. Either way, personal experience in and of itself is not sufficient to produce a convincing argument, for the latter will always be dependent on whose hands the experience falls. When the experience is one of epistemic injustice falling on the lives of children, it can go unnoticed, for such injustices deprive those children of the very tools necessary to articulate the experience (I discuss this in Chapter 4).

Most, if not all those who will read this book have never experienced being placed, during most of their school life and in plain view of others, in a 'low ability' group or class at school. They may have seen no problems with ability grouping practices, as they often saw themselves benefited by them (Preckel et al., 2019). The inside perspective as a child in 'low ability' groups is thus unreachable to us. And yet, we claim to know what we are talking about when we say that such practice is not only academically ineffective but emotionally damaging. We make the claim based on research, on behalf of vulnerable others, but not from personal experience. If nothing else, not being in a bottom set is by itself a boost to one's self-esteem.

Lacking personal experience can sometimes be a limitation for authors in the social sciences. Rightly or wrongly, we tend to listen more keenly to the voice of experience. To those who not only can articulate and support their arguments but who have also lived and breathed them, rather than to those who arrive at them purely through reading and reflection; the armchair philosopher. Politicians know this and are able to manipulate citizens through the right rhetoric accordingly (Runciman, 2018).

Although limiting oneself to reading and thinking are valuable experiences in themselves, when the object of such thoughts belongs to the realm of practical experience, something can be left wanting. The idea of 'being there', in itself is not enough either (Radford, 2022). I was there, as a classroom practitioner, interacting as one of the expected actors in a school, but this did not necessarily allow me to experience (by which I mean, feel) children's humiliation in the bottom sets, much like a warden who interacts with prisoners does not necessarily know what being a prisoner 'really feels like'. Being there however, does give us some insights, and for me it was the alarming understanding of what children in the United Kingdom are subjected to, to every stake holder's knowledge.

Although I was shocked to see children intellectually segregated in this way in the United Kingdom, it troubled me even more to see schools and teachers embrace the practice regardless of research evidence. Schools do not call it 'segregation' but 'grouping'. Apartheid in South Africa (1948–1994) was a form of racial segregation that would have been just as appalling had it been called 'people grouping'. To group children at school by their physical attributes (apart from age or gender in some cases) would be unthinkable, and yet, we group them according to their intellectual ability as if this brought no consequences worthy of concern.

At best, if we ever were, as children, the recipients of perceived injustices from adults, we may have the authority of reflecting on such experiences and any subsequent feelings of impotence, however briefly they may have been. If not necessarily to the bottom sets of ability, we all know what humiliation feels like; we've been to that place at least.

Concluding thoughts

The problem with never having been to this place, of never having experienced constant relegation to the bottom sets as academics, is that its negative impact goes mostly unnoticed, and its moral cause therefore, easily forgotten. The intellectual elites may complain about the 'unthinking crowds' and never see their own hand in it; their own share of the responsibility.

If we could allow children to live beyond ability labels—much like bell hooks (2012) wished to live beyond race—that would be a radical move indeed in education. This is not possible in the United States, United Kingdom, or any Western country that I can think of, other than, perhaps, in isolated examples of liberal education initiatives, like free Montessori schools, although these too have been found to lack more accessible enrolment processes (Debs and Brown, 2017). To live beyond ability labels may be difficult because, as Zelman and Sorensen observe, children's education is not built around the needs of children, but the needs of adults. As the eugenics movement demonstrated, in order to run an Empire its subjects needed to be purposely positioned as early as possible. Knowing who your subjects or citizens are; knowing their strengths and weaknesses and capitalizing on the former still seems to be paramount.

To insinuate that the Eugenics movement is in any way responsible for ability grouping practices may be seen as a step too far by some. I stand by this link however, not in terms of racial breeding but of the intellectual or academic creaming off that appears to take place. This is harmful to our society in the long run because, as Michael Young foretold, it gives the appearance of fairness, leaving those who 'cannot' make it disfranchised.

Bottom set children, low track children, either label is just as demoralizing for whoever bears it. Had I taught in the United States, this book could easily have been called 'Citizens of the Low Track'. It is no coincidence that both UK and US school systems practise ability grouping, and in sketching some relevant aspects of both countries, I seek only to allow the reader, from wherever they may be, an opportunity to map out and recognize aspects and implications of ability grouping, if there are any, in their own educational contexts.

References

Ansalone, G., & Biafora, F. A. (2010). Tracking in the schools: Perceptions and attitudes of parents. *Race, Gender & Class, 17*(1/2), 226–240.

Archer, L., Francis, B., Miller, S., Taylor, B., Tereshchenko, A., Mazenod, A., Pepper, D., & Travers, M.-C. (2018). The symbolic violence of setting: A Bourdieusian analysis of mixed methods data on secondary students' views about setting. *British Educational Research Journal, 44*(1), 119–140. https://doi.org/10.1002/berj.3321

Barnett, S. W., & Lamy, C. E. (2013). Achievement gaps start early: Preschool can help. In P. L. Carter & K. G. Welner (Eds.), *Closing the opportunity gap: What America must do to give every child an even chance*. Oxford University Press.

Boaler, J., Wiliam, D., & Brown, M. (2000). Students' experiences of ability grouping: Disaffection, polarisation and the construction of failure. *British Educational Research Journal, 26*(5), 631–648.

Bradbury, A., Braun, A., & Quick, L. (2021). Intervention culture, grouping and triage: High-stakes tests and practices of division in English primary schools. *British Journal of Sociology of Education, 42*(2), 147–163.

Brown Center on Education Policy. (2013). *The resurgence of ability grouping and persistence of tracking.*

Burris, C. C., & Garrity, D. T. (2008). *Detracking for excellence and equity*. ASCD.

Carter, P. L., & Welner, K. G. (Eds.). (2013). *Closing the opportunity gap: What America must do to give every child an even chance* (Illustrated edition). Oxford University Press.

Chakravorty, S. (2019). *The truth about us: The politics of information from Manu to Modi*. Hachette India.

Charlton, E., Mills, M., Martino, W., & Beckett, L. (2007). Sacrificial girls: A case study of the impact of streaming and setting on gender reform. *British Educational Research Journal*, *33*(4), 459–478.

Chisaka, B. C., & Vakalisa, N. C. G. (2003). Some effects of ability grouping in Harare secondary schools: A case study. *South African Journal of Education*, *23*(3), 176–180.

Chitty, C. (2009). IQ and eleven-plus selection. In *Eugenics, Race and Intelligence in Education*. Continuum.

Choudhury, R. A. (2015) *The forgotten children: The association of parents of backward children and the legacy of eugenics in Britain, 1946–1960*. ProQuest Dissertations Publishing.

Collie, R. J., & Mansfield, C. F. (2022). Teacher and school stress profiles: A multilevel examination and associations with work-related outcomes. *Teaching and Teacher Education*, *116*, 103759.

Cowan, D. (2020). James Brooke-Smith. Gilded Youth: Privilege, Rebellion and the British Public School. London: Reaktion Books, 2019. Pp. 296. $25.00 (cloth). *Journal of British Studies*, *59*(4), 932–933. https://doi.org/10.1017/jbr.2020.72

Debs, M., & Brown, K. E. (2017). Students of color and public Montessori schools: A review of the literature. *Journal of Montessori Research*, *3*(1), 1.

Dudley, E. (2015). *Mixed-ability teaching/Edmund Dudley and Erika Osváth*. Oxford University Press.

Francis, B., Taylor, B., Tereshchenko, A., Taylor, B., & Tereshchenko, A. (2019). *Reassessing 'ability' grouping: Improving practice for equity and attainment*. Routledge.

Fuligni, A. J., Eccles, J. S., & Barber, B. L. (1995). Long-term effects of seventh-grade ability grouping in mathematics. *The Journal of Early Adolescence*, *15*(1), 58–89.

Hajar, A. (2018). Exploring Year 6 pupils' perceptions of private tutoring: Evidence from three mainstream schools in England. *Oxford Review of Education*, *44*(4), 514–531.

Hallam, S., & Ireson, J. (2008). Subject domain differences in secondary school teachers' attitudes towards grouping pupils by ability. *Zbornik Instituta Za Pedagoška Istraživanja*, *40*(2), 369–387.

Hansen, B. (2008). Is the bluebird really a phoenix? Ability grouping seems to rise from the ashes ad infinitum. *Reading Today*, *25*(6), 19–20.

hooks, bell. (2012). Introduction: On reflection and lamentation. In *Appalachian elegy* (pp. 1–8). University Press of Kentucky (Poetry and Place).

Hove, N. (2022). The inclusiveness of mixed ability grouping in Johannesburg primary schools. *South African Journal of Childhood Education*, *12*(1), 1–9.

Kayumova, S., & Dou, R. (2022). Equity and justice in science education: Toward a pluriverse of multiple identities and onto-epistemologies. *Science Education, 106*(5), 1097–1117.

Kittay, E. F. (2019). On what matters/not. In E. F. Kittay (Ed.), *Learning from my daughter: The value and care of disabled minds* (p. 0). Oxford University Press.

Klassen, R. M. (2010). Teacher stress: The mediating role of collective efficacy beliefs. *The Journal of Educational Research (Washington, D.C.), 103*(5), 342–350.

Knoester, M., & Au, W. (2017). Standardized testing and school segregation: Like tinder for fire? *Race, Ethnicity and Education, 20*(1), 1–14.

Kosunen, S., Bernelius, V., Seppänen, P., & Porkka, M. (2020). School choice to lower secondary schools and mechanisms of segregation in urban Finland. *Urban Education (Beverly Hills, Calif.), 55*(10), 1461–1488.

Lareau, A. (2011). *Unequal childhoods: Class, race, and family life* (2nd ed.). University of California Press.

Limura, S. (2018). Stress-related growth in Japanese adolescents experiencing high school entrance examinations. *Current Psychology (New Brunswick, N.J.), 37*(4), 803–808.

Lowe, R. (2021). *Schooling and social change since 1760: Creating inequalities through education*. Routledge.

Luna, J. P., & Medel, R. M. (2023). Uneven States, unequal societies, and democracy's unfulfilled promises: Citizenship rights in Chile and contemporary Latin America. *Latin American Politics and Society, 65*(2), 170–196.

Martin, J. (2022). A chronological introduction. In J. Martin (Ed.), *Gender and education in England since 1770: A social and cultural history* (pp. 1–22). Springer International (Gender and History).

McGillicuddy, D., & Devine, D. (2020). "You feel ashamed that you are not in the higher group"—Children's psychosocial response to ability grouping in primary school. *British Educational Research Journal, 46*(3), 553–573.

McInerney, L. (2013). *What I learned from writing about grammar schools, Laura McInerney*. Retrieved November 18, 2023, from https://lauramcinerney.com/what-i-learned-from-writing-about-grammar-schools/

Medina, J., Benner, K., & Taylor, K. (2019). Actresses, business leaders and other wealthy parents charged in U.S. college entry fraud. *New York Times*, 12 March.

Murphy, J., & Hallinger, P. (1989). Equity as access to learning: Curricular and instructional treatment differences. *Journal of Curriculum Studies, 21*(2), 129–149.

Plowden, B. (1967). *Plowden report*. Retrieved February 16, 2021, from www.educationengland.org.uk/documents/plowden/plowden1967-1.html

Pomfret, D. M. (2015) *Youth and empire: Trans-colonial childhoods in British and French Asia*. Stanford University Press.

Preckel, F., Schmidt, I., Stumpf, E., Motschenbacher, M., Vogl, K., Scherrer, V., & Schneider, W. (2019). High-ability grouping: Benefits for gifted students' achievement development without costs in academic self-concept. *Child Development*, *90*(4), 1185–1201.
Radford, C. W. (2022). Enacting disruptive encounters. In *Lived experiences and social transformations* (pp. 192–227). Brill.
Reay, D. (2017). *Miseducation: Inequality, education and the working classes* (1st ed.). Policy Press. https://doi.org/10.2307/j.ctt22p7k7m
Reese, W. J. (2013). *Testing wars in the public schools a forgotten history/ William J. Reese*. Harvard University Press. https://doi.org/10.4159/harvard.9780674075672
Runciman, D. (2018). *Political hypocrisy: The mask of power, from Hobbes to Orwell and beyond*, Revised Edition – Second Edition/David Runciman. (Revised). Princeton University Press. https://doi.org/10.23943/9781400889662
Sacks, P. (1999). *Standardized minds: The high price of America's testing culture and what we can do to change it.* . Perseus Books.
Sandel, M. J. (2020). *The tyranny of merit: What's become of the common good?*. Allen Lane.
Silvers, A. (2009). Interactional differentiation in the mixed-ability group: A situated view of two struggling readers. Reading Research Quarterly, 43, 228–250. Deborah Poole, 2008. *TESOL Quarterly*, *43*(1), 150–151.
Spina, N. (2019). "Once upon a time": Examining ability grouping and differentiation practices in cultures of evidence-based decision-making. *Cambridge Journal of Education*, *49*(3), 329–348.
Stark, L. (2014). Naming giftedness: Whiteness and ability discourse in US schools. *International Studies in Sociology of Education*, *24*(4), 394–414.
Stone, D. (2002). *Breeding superman: Nietzsche, race and eugenics in Edwardian and Interwar Britain*. DGO-Digital original. Liverpool University Press.
Sykes, C. J. (1996). *Dumbing down our kids: Why American children feel good about themselves but can't read, write, or add* (2nd ed.). St. Martin's Griffin.
Tienken, C. H., & Zhao, Y. (2013). How common standards and standardized testing widen the opportunity gap. In P. L. Carter & K. G. Welner (Eds.), *Closing the opportunity gap: What America must do to give every child an even chance* (p. 0). Oxford University Press.
Tomlinson, C. A. (1999). *The differentiated classroom: Responding to the needs of all learners* (1st ed.). Association for Supervision & Curriculum Development.
Towers, E., Taylor, B., Tereshchenko, A., & Mazenod, A. (2019). "The reality is complex": Teachers' and school leaders' accounts and justifications of grouping practices in the English key stage 2 classroom. *Education 3–13*, *48*(1), 22–36.

Tyson, K. (2013). Tracking, segregation, and the opportunity gap: What we know and why it matters. In P. L. Carter & K. G. Welner (Eds.), *Closing the opportunity gap: What America must do to give every child an even chance* (pp. 169–180). Oxford University Press.

Venkatakrishnan, H., & Wiliam, D. (2003). Tracking and mixed-ability grouping in secondary school mathematics classrooms: A case study. *British Educational Research Journal, 29*(2), 189–204.

Welner, K. G., & Oakes, J. (1996). (Li)ability grouping: The new susceptibility of school tracking systems to legal challenges. *Harvard Educational Review, 66*(3), 451–470.

Wilkins, C. (2011). Professionalism and the post-performative teacher: New teachers reflect on autonomy and accountability in the English school system. *Professional Development in Education, 37*(3), 389–409.

Young. (2015). *Toby Young's genetic meritocracy.* Quadrant Online.

Zelman, S., & Sorensen, M. E. (2022). *The buying and selling of American education.* Rowman & Littlefield.

Zevenbergen, R. (2005). The construction of a mathematical habitus: Implications of ability grouping in the middle years. *Journal of Curriculum Studies, 37*(5), 607–619.

2 There is no democracy in childhood

Whose democracy?

The question of what constitutes an effective democracy is a complex and interdisciplinary endeavour (Christinao and Bajaj, 2022). Any normative definition I could present here might be soon contested and divert attention from my main concern. Suffice to say that the sort of democracy I would advocate for does not need the academic humiliation or debasement of its vulnerable citizens in order to function. If it does need it, it is a democracy whose moral conduct I would wish to improve. However, any appeals to moral conduct or values in democracies today encounter challenges from the culture of success, profit, and 'economicism' (Jover et al., 2018).

John Dewey's conception of democracy emphasizes the role of experience in the democratic process; it opens the door to the practical aspects of such experience in the classroom.

In his later works (1925–1953), Dewey revisits some of the ideas he first introduced in democracy and education. An important characteristic of democracy, says Dewey, is how each generation makes sense of what democracy can mean.

> Every generation has to accomplish democracy over again for itself; that its very nature, its essence, is something that cannot be handed on from one person or one generation to another, but has to be worked out in terms of needs, problems and conditions of the social life of which, as the years go by, we are a part, a social life that is changing with extreme rapidity from year to year ("Democracy and Education in the World of Today", 1938a).
>
> (in Hildebrand, 2023: 92)

DOI: 10.4324/9781003398202-3

This is why school education plays an important role in the shaping of citizens and the democracy they accomplish. However, how do we ensure that our children are, at least to some extent morally and ethically prepared for such endeavour?

The concept of what it means to be an 'informed citizen' begins at school. I will explore how schools fall short of giving children empowering experiences as members of a society that claims democratic principles. For example, in the United Kingdom such principles are:

1. Checks and balances—these prevent one person or group being too powerful.
2. Freedom of speech and association—different views can be aired, and political parties or groups can form and compete openly.
3. Free and fair elections—people can vote for who they want and can trust the outcome of elections.
4. Transparency and openness—people know who is responsible for decisions and can hold them to account.
5. Active participation by the public—elected representatives are kept in touch with the people they represent.

(UK Parliament, 2019)

I claim that ability grouping practices are not only unethical, but they also impede the transparent execution of such principles or warp our view of them. I do not take these principles up individually, but rather as an example of what 'democracy' means to some nations; that to grasp what each of these principles tackle requires an informed citizenry. It necessitates the *experience* of democracy and not just the understanding of a definition. Dewey thought that schools were well-placed to provide such beginnings; to provide,

> a mode of associated living, of conjoint communicated experience. The extension in space of the number of individuals who participate in an interest so that each has to refer his own action to that of others, and to consider the action of others to give point and direction to his own, is equivalent to the breaking down of those barriers of class, race, and national territory which kept men from perceiving the full import of their activity.
>
> (Dewey, 1916: 101)

Thus, I start with childhood. Not in terms of other people's children—or even our own children, but of our own experiences of childhood. We all felt the vulnerability of that first day at school, unsure of our place in it. How we were treated by adults became our first lesson.

Remembering one's childhood

I learned to appraise the world differently when I came across critical realism (Bhaskar et al., 1998). It allowed me to understand phenomena in all their complex, interplaying aspects and realities. For instance, to think of childhood is to consider the child as an infant human being, but also as abstract symbols of immaturity, inadequacy or deficiency, vulnerability, potentiality, playfulness, innocence, etc. There is also the perspective from childhood itself; the child in fear, wonder, trouble, boredom, or awe; the child as an egocentric being; the child as small in stature and of weak constitution (compared to adults); the child in experience (the unconscious giver) of unconditional love, of everlasting and passing friendships and foes; the child in school, in class, and in homework; the child during breaktime or at home, on the street or backyard, as playfellows, moving between danger and safety, real or virtual, etc.; and the child within. All and more of such aspects are part of childhood. To focus on one disregarding another is to get a partial look, or to look inattentively. Children inhabit these aspects constantly, in no set order, now suppressing some, now indulging others. Thus, their academic or intellectual work mingles with their social and emotional lives inextricably, moderating each other. The 'good' of one will not necessarily be the 'good' of the other. Some of the challenges in a child's life lie hidden at such intersections.

How do we write about childhood experiences as adults? I often ask my trainee teachers to remember themselves as school children; to imagine themselves at their table, beholding the new teacher as he or she enters the classroom, where this teacher is in fact, their own selves as adult. I ask them to remember some misdemeanour, any injustices or any moments of achievement they had as school children and share them if they feel they can. I share mine with them. For instance, when I was eight, I was punished for having repeatedly moved around, disturbing others' work (apparently). I say 'apparently' because I remember asking around for colour pens, glue, scissors, and paper (I hadn't brought my own for some reason). The punishment was for me to bring myself and my desk to the front of the class, right up to the board, which was humiliating. I do recall asking around for the materials, but I do not recall having done so repeatedly, nor do I recall disturbing others' work. I assume I was given warnings not to do these things. As I would later learn, 'To keep the eyes on the book and the ears open to the teacher's words is a mysterious source of intellectual grace' (Dewey, 1916: 166) I did not appear to have. I was told off. Now, had they asked me *why* I disobeyed the teacher, *why* I kept leaving my desk and disturbing others, my answer would have been, 'I don't know'. For they would be asking me about things I was not aware of having done. 'I don't know' is a very common answer children give adults which they seldom give each other. Adults always seem to ask the wrong questions.

We all have memories of our school days that we should reflect on when entering the teaching profession. Whether teachers end up teaching in the way they were trained to teach or in the way they themselves were taught as children has been debated (Olitsky, 2013; Cox, 2014; Brown et al., 2021). But reflecting on one's educational experiences can help us understand how others' experiences differ. As adults we can challenge our own childhood memories; we can critique, for instance, our childhood equanimity regarding ability grouping. If we were placed in the 'high ability' sets, we can challenge our belief that it was the right thing to do; that we should have felt good about being there, etc.

Initial thoughts on John Dewey's writings on experience, democracy, and education

Some of John Dewey's ideas regarding the role of education in the making of a citizen are central to my argument. Since his publications which ranged from 1884 to 1949, much has been written in great depth and perspectives about his contribution to such issues (Saito, 2005; Bernstein, 2010; Quay and Seaman, 2013; Westbrook, 2015; Heilbronn et al., 2018, etc.). Every generation sees Dewey through slightly different eyes, adjusting interpretations accordingly, and yet, to anyone involved in education, there is much to be found in his original thoughts still. One example is how Dewey viewed education as implicit in the act of growing, which underlies his philosophy of democracy and education. He proclaims: 'Education is all one with growing; it has no end beyond itself' (DE, 54). The aim of education, for Dewey, is to produce more growth in a child, to foster a continuous reorganization of a child's experience in his or her interaction with the adult world. From a purely utilitarian viewpoint the critique has been, to grow into what exactly? What is the endpoint or product of this growth? But Dewey's idea is one of growth without fixed ends, let alone profitable ends. This makes some sense in the age of the knowledge economy, where workers and professionals need to be constantly updating and growing their knowledge base, which in higher education leads ultimately to an economizing logic of profit and loss (Livingstone and Guile, 2012), rather than to the unmeasurable and ever-evolving growth of the person as a citizen. The ideas of growing without fixed ends does not imply that we do not earn a living, or that having a job is the end of our growth.

The role of reflective thought occasioned by experience in education is usually exemplified by Dewey in how we can engage children through real life problems, by making the curriculum relatable to the child's experiences. This, he says, moves us forward as whole persons and not merely as pupils. In Aristotelian fashion, knowledge and understanding are inseparable from the real problems of common life. The artificial, subject-related problems posed by a teacher (i.e. pretending you are ordering French food at a French restaurant) are not really the child's problem, 'or rather, they are his only as a pupil, not as a human being' (Dewey, 1916: 183). The real-life problem of the child thus becomes how to satisfy, or seem to satisfy, the teacher's wishes, school-life requirements, parental or peer expectations;

> how to come near enough to meeting them to slide along without an undue amount of friction.
>
> (ibid, 183)

Here is where I position my argument in terms of where the child's real problems—his own problems—in school lie, for instance, how children navigate the *personal experiences* that school-life gives them, on a day-to-day basis, as when grouped by ability.

The child as emergent citizen within schools' autocratic system

Children are usually excluded from decision pertaining to their education. They are deemed immature to make pedagogical or curriculum decisions. Thus, they seldom experience a sense of emergent citizenry at home or at school, except in their play, and even there things do not always run smoothly (i.e. bullying). Autocracy, therefore, is what most of us, as children, learned to survive. The sort of citizen that autocracy occasions is either an instrumentalist and ideologically aligned citizen, or a despondent or rebellious one, depending on how the child was able to navigate their experiences.

An autocratic system however, does not exclude the possibility of asking, listening and taking on board children's opinions; it does not mean that their experience of school life, as persons, is not relevant to our decision making. If we take a holistic approach to democracy, as experienced through education, we can better integrate all parties concerned, not as a favour or indulgence, but as a right and astute move.

Woods (2017) suggests a move away from ideology and instrumentalism in democracy. He observes,

> Holistic democracy describes a way of working together which facilitates the growth and learning of individuals as whole people (meaning), as well as co-responsibility, mutual empowerment and fair participation of all in co-creating their social and organisational environment (participation).
>
> (Woods, 2017: 11)

Critics might say that a wholistic democracy at school would occasion a utopian citizen. That is to say, the capitalist and neo-liberal systems that feed individualistic concerns would not approve of such a socially oriented move, and would therefore describe it as wishful thinking at best, or a road to communism or anarchism at worst, as is often declared in political campaigns. However, ability grouping practices place individualistic concerns above the common good, as well as consider the concerns and common good of some, above the concerns and common good of everyone.

Most governments see the purpose of school education primarily as that of the transmission and acquisition of subject knowledge, with reading, writing, and arithmetic as central focus. What is read and written about, however, is usually up to the school. In my many years of observing primary school teachers, little is made of this opportunity for innovative content. Despite the use of some outstanding storybooks that deal with difference and discrimination (in whatever shape or form), such gestures are exceptions that prove the rule, and never get translated into whole school debates that could lead to structural change; they are left at the 'day' or 'month' level at most, as in Black History Month (Beamont, 1997; Doharty, 2019; Brill, 2021). Thus, in the autocratic school, hidden agendas come to the surface through the organization of teaching and learning, allowing children to experience duplicity indirectly, where school's discourse does not always reflect schools' actions.

Greta Thunberg: no school today

Young children are not known for their political empowerment, but teenagers like Greta Thunberg appear to understand all too well how citizenry cannot be enacted effectively inside school. At age 15 in 2018, Greta would 'play truant' every Friday and sit in front of the Swedish parliament, protesting and demanding immediate action on climate change. As Verharen (2021) suggests, Greta Thunberg would be Nietzsche's 'poster child', in that she represents youth's emancipation from and challenge to the older generation inside school by refusing to attend, and outside school by demanding politicians' attention. In her autobiography, No One Is Too Small to Make a Difference (Thunberg, 2019a), Greta develops her address to the adult world, 'We've come here to let you know that change is coming whether you like it or not' (Thunberg, 2019 b, UN speech). Not only did she know that her voice of protest and democratic agency could only be effective outside of school, but the very act (misdemeanour) of missing school was essential to her message. She could not be an empowered, 'proper citizen' inside the school gates.

There seems to be a natural learning flow in the life of human beings that schools prosaically interrupt in terms of their organization and environment. Such flow, Dewey argued, influences the mental and moral dispositions of children towards experience. Greta was allowed (supported) to be critical of school's concerns by not attending it; her moral and impassioned sentiments were clearly related to issues outside of school and in which school had little say. Fridays, thus, became the day where school was in fact shamed for being completely inadequate to enact one's citizenship.

Greta, however, is an exception that proves the rule. Few 11–16 year-olds feel politically motivated to miss school in protest. Another exception is the 2006 mass, and still ongoing street protests and school occupations[1] of secondary school children in Chile (Paiva, 2021), who demand a more equitable education.

There is no democracy in childhood 39

As future citizens of a democracy, children's mental and moral dispositions ought to matter. One of the aims of the school environment, says Dewey, is to integrate the many other environments children inhabit (family, community, religion, etc.), adding a wider and therefore more balanced environment that can inform children's actions. This cannot be achieved through any one particular subject, but through the way in which schools choose to structure their educative aims. Thus,

> the only way in which adults consciously control the kind of education which the immature get is by controlling the environment in which they *act*, and hence *think* and *feel*. We never educate directly, but indirectly by means of the environment.
>
> (Dewey, 1916: 27, my italics)

Teaching citizenship for instance, either discreetly or through the social sciences, will be ineffective if other more powerful school practices and environment, like ability grouping, are at work.

> if schools continue to promote one set of values through their taught curriculum but promote contradictory values through their leadership practice, they undermine the legitimacy of democracy; worse, moral inconsistency and double standards are legitimised and normalised.
>
> (Orchard, 2012: 223)

Initiatives around 'character formation', 'growth mindset', or 'citizenship' for example, are not learned by children discreetly, but through other, tacit school practices (Shepperd et al., 2011). In other words, citizenship is contextually learned through the way the teaching organization is taken up, which reflects the values of a society (Biesta, 2010). Similarly, growth mindset, which entails the 'belief that personal characteristics, such as intellectual abilities, can be developed' (Yeager and Dweck, 2020: 1270), like moral dispositions, is not exercised through instruction, but through experience. If we want children to become conscientious citizens, less prone to being manipulated within a democracy, we must educate them by providing environments that encourage epistemic virtue (love of learning) as a collective good, whatever their personal abilities, and 'not only in our minds and imaginations, but in reality' (Durkheim, 1961: 251).

In such a case, and to return to this book's overarching concern, ability grouping practices within the schools' autocratic system, foster neither epistemic virtue nor the idea of a collective good. Practices that encourage self-preservation and submission at one end, and indifference or rebelliousness at the other, are unlikely to lead to social cohesion and transparent democratic processes.

Children's rights

We know that grouping adults by ability (not roles) within an institution is not something we could contemplate for ourselves, even if it were for our own academic good. What sort of 'good' is this therefore, that sits so comfortably when applied to childhood? For example, adults would not tolerate being sent to bed early, even if there were good reasons for doing so. We make children go to bed early (in many countries), so that they may be alert and ready for school the following morning. Children often complain, but we do it for their own good, and studies show as much—if studies were needed to convince anyone. And there's the rub. Sometimes studies are not enough to convince anyone, because something stronger is driving belief and practice.

Approximately 95% of peer reviewed literature shows that grouping children by ability not only fails to achieve its promise of progress for all, but is in fact harmful to some children's ongoing learning experience and self-esteem. Much has been compellingly said already (Kutnick et al., 2005; Gillard, 2008; Marks, 2016; Francis et al., 2019; Towers et al., 2019; Bradbury et al., 2021). And yet, as Priscilla Alderson (2016) observes, childhood studies do not function as emancipatory tools for children. What sort of convincing do we need to stop ability grouping practices, particularly when so many are already convinced of the 'good' in it? Therefore, what sort of 'good' is this?

Is it the sort of good Alice Miller referred to in her 1983 book, when she wrote about the everyday violence many children used to suffer in the name of good-old-fashioned discipline, and of what she called 'poisonous pedagogies'? The kind that ended with '*You'll thank me one day*', '*I do this for your own good*', '*It hurts me more than it hurts you*', etc.? Is it that kind of good? The one that needs no research?

Many children internalize the identities that adults give them, for how could adults mean them harm?

As Miller observed, the danger of having suffered harm in childhood is twofold: that we may excuse it and that we may perpetrate it on others,

> When people who have been beaten or spanked as children attempt to play down the consequences by setting themselves up as examples, even claiming it was good for them, they are inevitably contributing to the continuation of cruelty in the world by this refusal to take their childhood tragedies seriously.
>
> (Miller, 1990, xiii)

If we were taught not to take our own childhood tragedies seriously, how can we possibly even recognize the tragedy of others? If we consider our own tragic childhood experiences as a norm, then we will seek validation by ensuring this norm is sustained for others.

Children will seldom protest. All advocacy related to children's lives and rights is usually done by adults. Thus, any emancipatory act of childhood is an act of advocacy; a kind of childhood hindsight; adults who once were children (past members), acting on behalf of the experience of being a child, and becoming aware of how this experience is shaped:

> children learn about persons by finding out what responsive activities these persons exact and what these persons will do in reply to the children's activities.
>
> (Dewey, 1916: 317)

The Children Rights Convention therefore is a product of adults' reflection on childhood and society. The convention however has been ratified by 145 countries, *excepting* the United States and Somalia, with Britain having a tokenistic approach which has been continuously criticized in reviews held by the Committee on the Rights of the Child. In 2004, Alderson had already observed that,

> Before we can have education for democracy in democratic schools we have to correct the misperceptions based on myths that children and young people are so very different from adults. And also that somehow they benefit from, or do not realise, or do not mind, being treated so disrespectfully.
>
> (Alderson, 2004: 3)

Alderson also observed, 'mainstream research ignores children, much as it used to ignore women, and academic texts seldom mention children' (Alderson, 2016: 201). We see children's agency as not individually located but rather socially situated (Oswell, 2013), hence the group(s) children belong to affects their sense of agency. Bearing this in mind, it is no wonder to find practice in education that is contrary to some of the statements found in articles in the Convention on the Rights of the Child (1990), particularly in articles 2, 3, and 29.

Article 2.2 states that children ought to be,

> protected against all forms of discrimination or punishment on the basis of the status, activities, expressed opinions, or beliefs of the child's parents, legal guardians, or family members.

This is compounded by the fact that most children in 'low ability' groups come from disadvantaged groups already (low economic status, limited situated cultural capital, refugee families, etc.).

Article 3.1 states that,

> In all actions concerning children, ... the best interests of the child shall be a primary consideration.

This of course will depend on what is understood by 'best interest'. As I have suggested, focusing only on intellectual and academic abilities does not serve the best interest of the whole child, and certainly not of the society in which they will live.

Article 29.1.a states,

> the education of the child shall be directed to the development of the child's personality, talents and mental and physical abilities to their fullest potential.

This is probably the most infracted of rights, for in ability grouping practices it serves only a few children at the expense of the rights of the many. What the research shows time and time again is that ability grouping actively narrows the academic horizons of children deemed 'less able'. And yet, the practice is still embraced.

Concluding thoughts

To remember one's school days is to put oneself momentarily in a place of vulnerability. As adults, we can revisit this place differently, and consider how our young self, away from parents, was shaped into the citizen today; what values were encouraged through our school experiences. How schools structure the child's learning and participatory environment will influence children as emergent citizens.

On whose behalf is our sense of 'good' performed around ability grouping? I take this question up in the next chapter. But it seems to me that the experience of going to school, as it is now, cannot encourage conscientious citizens, for there is indeed, no experience of democracy in childhood, only plenty of talk at best.

Note

1 Students take command of the school gates and interior, not allowing anyone in or out until the protest is over.

References

Alderson, P. (2004). Democracy in schools: Myths, mirages and making it happen. In B. Linsley & E. Rayment (Eds.), *Beyond the classroom: Exploring active citizenship in 11–16 education*. New Politics Network.

Alderson, P. (2016). The philosophy of critical realism and childhood studies. *Global Studies of Childhood*, 6(2), 199–210.

Beamon, T. (1997, February 20). A Black History Month obligation or celebration?; African Americans question whether observance has become just another uninspired routine: FINAL edition. *Washington Post*, D, 3:1.

Bernstein, R. J. (2010). Dewey's vision of radical democracy. In M. Cochran (Ed.), *The Cambridge companion to Dewey* (pp. 288–308). Cambridge University Press.

Bhaskar, R., Archer, M., Collier, A., Lawson, T., & Norrie, A. (Eds.). (1998). *Critical realism: Essential readings*. Routledge.

Biesta, G. J. J. (2010). Why 'what works' still won't work: From evidence-based education to value-based education. *Studies in Philosophy and Education*, 29(5), 491–503.

Bradbury, A., Braun, A., & Quick, L. (2021). Intervention culture, grouping and triage: High-stakes tests and practices of division in English primary schools. *British Journal of Sociology of Education*, 42(2), 147–163. https://doi.org/10.1080/01425692.2021.1878873

Brill, E. (2021). "Early Childhood Education" and "Black History Month". *Radical Teacher*, *121*, 109–111,113.

Brown, C. P., Barry, D. P., Ku, D. H., & Puckett, K. (2021). Teach as I say, not as I do: How preservice teachers made sense of the mismatch between how they were expected to teach and how they were taught in their professional training program. *Teacher Educator*, *56*(3), 250–269.

Christiano, T., & Bajaj, S. (2022). Democracy. In E. N. Zalta (Ed.), *The Stanford encyclopedia of philosophy* (Spring 2022). Metaphysics Research Lab, Stanford University. https://plato.stanford.edu/archives/spr2022/entries/democracy/

Cox, S. E. (2014). *Perceptions and influences behind teaching practices: Do teachers teach as they were taught?* ProQuest Dissertations Publishing.

Dewey, J. (1916). *Democracy and education*. Retrieved August 12, 2023, from http://archive.org/details/in.ernet.dli.2015.274992

Doharty, N. (2019). 'I FELT DEAD': Applying a racial microaggressions framework to Black students' experiences of Black History Month and Black History. *Race, Ethnicity and Education*, *22*(1), 110–129.

Durkheim, É. (1961). *Moral education: A study in the theory and application of the sociology of education / Foreword by Paul Fauconnet. Translated by Everett K. Wilson and Herman Schnurer. Edited, with an introd., by Everett K. Wilson.* Free Press of Glencoe.

Francis, B., Taylor, B., Tereshchenko, A., Taylor, B., & Tereshchenko, A. (2019). *Reassessing 'ability' grouping: Improving practice for equity and attainment.* Routledge. https://doi.org/10.4324/9780429436512

Gillard, D. (2008). *Us and them: A history of pupil grouping policies in England's schools. Education in England.* www.educationengland.org.uk/articles/27grouping.html

Heilbronn, R., Doddington, C., & Higham, R. (2018). *Dewey and education in the 21st century: Fighting back*. Emerald.

Hildebrand, D. (2023). John Dewey. In E. N. Zalta & U. Nodelman (Eds.), *The Stanford encyclopedia of philosophy* (Fall 2023). Metaphysics Research Lab, Stanford University. https://plato.stanford.edu/archives/fall2023/entries/dewey/

Jover, G., Martín, R. G., & Fuentes, J. L. (2018). Constructing creative democracy at school by reading the classics: A dialogue between Martha Nussbaum and John Dewey. In R. Heilbronn, C. Doddington, & R. Higham (Eds.), *Dewey and education in the 21st century* (pp. 61–79). Emerald Publishing Limited. https://doi.org/10.1108/978-1-78743-625-120181010

Kutnick, P., Sebba, J., Blatchford, P., Galton, M., & Thorp, J. (2005). *The effects of pupil grouping: Literature review.* (688; Department of Education and Skills). University of Brighton.

Livingstone, D. W., & Guile, D. (2012). Section one. In D. W. Livingstone & D. Guile (Eds.), *The knowledge economy and lifelong learning: A critical reader* (pp. 3–5). Sense Publishers.

Marks, R. (2016). *Children put in the bottom maths group at primary believe they'll never be any good*. The Conversation. http://theconversation.com/children-put-in-the-bottom-maths-group-at-primary-believe-theyll-never-be-any-good-54502

Olitsky, S. (2013). We teach as we are taught: Exploring the potential for emotional climate to enhance elementary science preservice teacher education. *Cultural Studies of Science Education*, 8(3), 561–570.

Orchard, J. L. (2012). *Good educational leadership: Principles of democratic practice: With reference to maintained schools in England*. Institute of Education, University of London.

Oswell, D. (2013). *The agency of children: From family to global human rights / David Oswell*. University Press.

Paiva, M. O. V. (2021). *The failed promise of neoliberal education: Social class and the making of youth futures in Concepcion, Chile*. ProQuest Dissertations Publishing.

Quay, J., & Seaman, J. (2013). *John Dewey and education outdoors: Making sense of the 'Educational Situation' through more than a century of progressive reforms*. Birkhäuser Boston.

Saito, N. (2005). *The gleam of light: Moral perfectionism and education in Dewey and Emerson / Naoko Saito*. Fordham University Press.

Sheppard, S., Ashcraft, C., & Larson, B. E. (2011). Controversy, citizenship, and counterpublics: Developing democratic habits of mind. *Ethics and Education*, 6(1), 69–84.

Thunberg, G. (2019a). *No one is too small to make a difference*. Penguin Books.

Thunberg, G. (2019b). If world leaders choose to fail us, my generation will never forgive them. *The Guardian*. www.theguardian.com/commentisfree/2019/sep/23/world-leaders-generation-climate-breakdown-greta-thunberg

Towers, E., Taylor, B., Tereshchenko, A., & Mazenod, A. (2019). 'The reality is complex': Teachers' and school leaders' accounts and justifications of grouping practices in the English key stage 2 classroom. *Education 3-13*, 48(1), 22–36. https://doi.org/10.1080/03004279.2019.1569707

UNICEF. (1990). *Convention on the Rights of the Child text*. Retrieved February 2, 2024, from www.unicef.org/child-rights-convention/convention-text

Verharen, C. C. (2021). Die Überkinder: Nietzsche and Greta Thunberg, children and philosophy. *Journal of Philosophy of Education*, 55(4–5), 878–892.

Westbrook, R. B. (2015). *John Dewey and American Democracy / Robert B. Westbrook*. Cornell University Press.

Woods, P. A. (2017). Researching holistic democracy in schools. *Democracy and Education*, 25(1).

Yeager, D. S., & Dweck, C. S. (2020). What can be learned from growth mindset controversies? *American Psychologist*, 75(9), 1269–1284.

3 Meritocracy and its allegiance to the empire

The idea that '*The habit of Empire is persistent*', a line from the film Dr, No (1962) used by Prasch (2005), helps me emphasize the fact that, even though neo-liberalist agendas are taken up by most countries in the globalized economy, only Britain maintains a hierarchy (a monarchy in fact) that permeates society with imperial values, allowing practices like ability grouping to appear '*common-sense*'. National awards that celebrate pioneering, innovation, and contribution (each double-edged concepts) still bear the word Empire (MBE, OBE) which suggests that, in terms of values, we still live in a kind of British empire today. The word 'British' and its colonial/imperial connotations in discourse, particularly in the context of 'Fundamental British Values' which schools are asked to adhere to, is another example that helps support imperial (colonial) practices. I contend that all this serves to implicitly support the idea that in the United Kingdom it still matters *to know one's place and the place of others*, and that therefore, grouping children by ability, though questionable outside the empire, is nothing surprising within it.

Why failure is your own fault

In his much celebrated and misunderstood book, *The rise of the meritocracy* (1994), Michael Young sets forth the idea of the dystopian society that meritocratic values could ultimately lead to. A society where,

> Intelligence has been redistributed between the classes, and the nature of the classes changed. The talented have been given the

opportunity to rise to the level which accords with their capacities, and the lower classes consequently reserved for those who are also lower in ability.

(Young, 1994: Intro)

This already happens in schools that group pupils by ability. The new intellectual elite that schools produce through meritocratic practices, leave behind a much larger community of dejected and academically rejected individuals, left to believe that they could have done better or that they simply lacked the ability to do so.

The concept of meritocracy escaped Young's original (1958) satirical vein and came to represent instead a positive ideal in society and particularly in education. Namely, those who succeed merit their success and can move up to the possibility of greater success; those who fail merit their failure. Although Young saw merit as the result of IQ + effort, it is not an 'effortocracy' that takes place in schools, for the focus is on the success of the individual and not necessarily on the effort employed or required. Young's son, Toby Young, believes that his father may not have been far off the mark when stating that meritocracy would be entirely achieved in the United Kingdom, in the shape of a cognitive elite, by 2033. In a hopeful vein he concludes,

All things being equal, a country's economy should grow faster, its public services should be run more efficiently, its politicians should make better decisions, diseases should be eradicated faster, and so on, if the people at the top possess the highest IQs and make the most effort.

(Young, 2020: 395)

However, human cognitive ability has no predetermined moral disposition. In fact, immoral or unethical actions that come from someone with a high IQ are highly questionable, for they cannot claim ignorance or lack of judgement (Minerd, 2018). For Young, merit and any effort required is viewed entirely in terms of cognitive capacity. It may be that Young felt morality was implicit in someone's high IQ, but historical atrocities show us that this is simply not the case (Jarausch, 2013). What is missing from Michael Young's equation is any sense of moral or ethical standards, let alone any element of compassion. In other words, there is no merit in kindness. Any fool can be kind and compassionate. Any fool (in many cases it's seen as 'only a fool') can give everything they are and have to others. Kindness and compassion, unlike money or cognitive abilities, are unmeasurable and self-denying, and therefor useless to a neo-liberal nation that holds steadfastly to its imperial power.

Inequality and inequity appear to be much more manageable when they can be directly attributed to the individual, as is the case with meritocratic practices,

> The discourse of meritocracy transfers responsibility for success or failure on individual learners, and inculcates a naive faith in the redemption of 'moving up' [sets]. In Foucauldian terms, this can be seen as an exemplification of governmentality, whereby individual subjects (in this case, pupils) actively interpolate the discourses that regulate them and 'buy in' to these processes of self-governance that then require no coercion.
> (Francis et al., 2019: 82)

However, the practice of ability grouping requires no coercion from schools or teachers either, as the culture of coercive compliance (Wilkins, 2011) also becomes internalized by practitioners (structural injustices). The Foucauldian term 'governmentality' is a neologism containing the terms, 'government' and 'rationality',

> This word [government] must be allowed the very broad meaning it had in the sixteenth century. 'Government' did not refer only to political structures or to the management of states; rather, it designated the way in which the *conduct* of individuals or of groups might be directed—the government of children, of souls, of communities, of the sick ... *To govern, in this sense, is to control the possible field of action of others.*
> (Sokhi-Bulley, 2014: par4)

The 'exemplification of governmentality' that Francis et al.'s referred to earlier, rightly equates with the discourse of meritocracy, tied to notions of a 'natural order' that legitimizes children's place in society, particularly children of wealthy parents. Ability grouping practices thus 'are signifiers within discourses of standards and "natural" distinction that constitute technologies of privilege' (Francis et al., 2017: 10).

Like most of the research, Francis et al.' study focuses on the disadvantaged segments of society, disproportionally represented in 'lower ability' groups. I believe that this focus does not lend strength to their argument, for regardless of how privileged a child is, he or she may well be in the 'lower ability' groups of their private school. We may argue that the harm done is cushioned by the wealth, but to do so is to agree and support ability grouping practices in certain contexts. If wealthier parents see that only economically disadvantaged children are the focus of research, why should they pay any heed or push for change in their own contexts? The humiliation experienced by being labelled as 'low ability' can be felt by anyone, rich or poor.

The notion of requiring no coercion to willingly participate in ability grouping practices is only partly explained by a belief in meritocracy; the false promise of a meritocracy where social inequalities are legitimized as 'justly deserved, and misfortune [as] personal failure' (Mijs, 2016: 26). Most countries organize their education system on a meritocratic basis without the use of ability grouping. The issue in schools that do, does not reside in knowing that someone else is better at something than I am, but in knowing that I am treated worse than others on that account.

In countries where children are constantly internally tested (weekly or fortnightly) and given grades, merit is often but a number that relates to memory power. It assumes that those who succeed have either put in the effort (to remember) and/or have an innate ability (or good memory) to succeed at that particular task. In this respect, one of the most enlightened practices in UK schools is the use of formative rather than summative assessment. Teachers give children verbal or written feedback on their learning rather than a summative number/grade. In other countries, the pressure of constant internal testing children experience cannot be stressed enough, but it is of a different nature to the stress that ability grouping occasions, for the latter carries an element of constant, visible humiliation. Children can hide and even forget a bad grade, but they cannot hide the daily experience of being placed in the 'low-ability' group/class, whatever the euphemism used (Giraffes, Triangles, etc.). Why are they there? Meritocracy will have us believe it is because they deserve to. The internalization of meritocratic practices makes teachers and parents believe that being in the bottom set or ability group is the child's best place. Children in higher sets are led to believe their peers' plight is their own fault, for not putting in the effort or simply for lacking the ability. The fact that most children in bottom sets come from disadvantaged backgrounds (Reay, 2017) is not seen as suspect enough to stop the practice. In any case, being in the 'low ability' group due to a disadvantaged background might be preferable to being there because of cognitive limitations. The former at least can be surmounted. Being singled out for being poor can be depersonalized, for it is not a child's fault to be poor, and such circumstances might change. Being singled out for lack of academic cognitive ability on the other hand, is a much deeper cut, for it is an attack on self, inherently and unbearably personal, like being singled out for the colour of our skin. Rich or poor, there is no hiding from it.

The habit of empire: neo-liberalism and empires today

There is a reason why the film character Darth Vader in Star Wars, leads an empire and not a republic. Empires conjure up ideas of injustice, tyranny, expansion at any cost, transgressions, greed, human rights violations, war, lack of empathy, etc. Notions of kindness, compassion, and justice seem to oppose notions of empire. With the advent of democracy, recent empires were quick to change their garb in order to keep their essence. The term 'neo-liberal nation' seemed like a sanitized expression, a name under which the British empire, as well as the 'American Empire' (Immerwahr, 2019) could continue their business, unimpeded (Shlaim, 2021).

It is not surprising therefore, that the habit of empire is persistent. But how is this habit instantiated exactly? The sociologist Michael Foucault (1979) explored how power began to be exerted over others through 'the gaze', particularly during the age of the French and British empires. The gaze is what allows the observation of others' behaviour, and hence, allows for their control. Foucault used as a metaphor the Panopticon, a new kind of prison invented by the 18th-century English philosopher Jeremy Bentham. The panopticon is an octagonal building with prison cells around all its periphery, with an observation tower in the centre. As all the cells face the centre, the guards need only look around to see any of the cells at any given time. The trick is to make the prisoners feel potentially, constantly observed (gazed at), even when no guard is present. This gaze, claims Foucault, is ultimately internalized by the prisoner. In other words, the prisoner ends up observing (checking) his own behaviour just in case he is in fact being observed by the guard. In a similar way, we check our daily behaviour in order to remain within the norms and values that the society in which we live upholds. The gaze of the empire is what unites all its subjects on a common pursuit: the acquisition of more power, be this financial or intellectual, in order to control more resources and technologies. The gaze conceals the values of empire, by making us believe that the whole world acts (or ought to act) in a similar way to the 'civilized' us.

It was the introduction of the concept of Fundamental British Values[1] (FBV), that crystalized for me the connection between meritocracy and empire, and thus the reasons why grouping by ability can seem to be a common-sense practice in British and most English-speaking cultures.

The need to uphold FBV is how the UK government responded to the perceived threat of Islamic extremism at the school level. The issue is, however, that in the choice of words the government conflates British national identity with democratic values (Crawford, 2017), and thus, I would argue, unintentionally uncovers the reason why the practice of grouping by ability seems common-sense, the demonym 'British' promoting the idea of empire and imperial values, rather than democracy and equality (or even meritocracy).

If we were to draw up a list, *judged by deeds* not rhetoric, of what would constitute 'Fundamental Roman Values', what values would such a list include? Would *respect* and *tolerance* come naturally to feature among them? Even though the word 'empire' has been omitted from my question, it is very hard to disentangle it from the word Roman, or, I would claim, from the word British. By the same token, certain attributes are distinctly attached to the idea of empire: expansion, conquest, invasion, subjugation, oppression, slavery, exploitation, order, profit, etc. The term 'British' (in 'British values') is too heavily compromised with its colonial past to evoke anything other than imperial values. The hierarchy at play, which often sees those at the bottom humiliated can seem to be a matter of course that fits in particularly well with meritocratic practices. This highlights the very problem with values; what feels right or seen as common-sense appears to need no justification based on reasoning or evidence. Thus, it may 'feel right' to categorize and subsequently segregate children by ability to maximize resources, even though the only beneficiaries are some children in the top sets.

Referring to the American education system, Kumashiro (2015) reminds us that going against common-sense is sometimes the only way to challenge oppressive educational practices. But who, within the empire, can gaze at the empire with different eyes? It is very difficult and ultimately unlikely that those who inhabit the values of empire will be able to see the harm done to others on its behalf, probably because many of them have been either beneficiaries wishing to keep their privileges, or victims needing to validate their experiences in some way. To suddenly see the invalidity of one's educational experiences; that we have been treated unfairly in our education, is to interrogate the empire. It means to contemplate a fight with a Goliath; to meet the imperial gaze and decide one's future path, for or against it. It seems much easier to tag along and to do to others what has been done to us.

A note on common-sense

If we are to examine how Britain judges success; who, for instance, among its citizens merit distinction or reward, what are we to make of such honours as the Order of the British Empire (OBE) or Member of the British Empire (MBE)[2] medals? Such language partly discloses the foundations on which the values of a nation (empire) grow. Imperial values are thus evoked and connected to pioneering spirit, to merit, to great success, and to winners as opposed to failure (not coming first, let alone coming last). Meritocracy in this respect has been the empire's most effective modus operandi for it keeps the hierarchies of power in place.

The 'natural order' that Francis et al.'s referred to earlier uses a Foucauldian lens to speak to the core values of certain societal groups, in their case the wealthy parents deploying all sort of resources to get the best and most privileged education for their children, thus keeping that 'natural order' of things. Their account however stops short of exploring things further. Many of those in privileged financial positions often make reference to the order of things by quoting even the Bible: 'You will always have the poor among you',[3] which presumably gives the powerful licence to be rich, intelligent, beautiful, etc., for we can easily exchange the word 'poor' with 'low ability' or 'ugly'. Nothing can be done about the order of things (apparently, for some), and this allows them to continue their rich, intelligent, or beautiful lives with an easy conscience, regardless of what the biblical text may have actually meant (Wafawanaka, 2014). My point being, that the 'natural order' appears thus to have a divine seal of approval, with kingship and godliness often interlinked in the background (Bryson, 2004; Cruz-Medina, 2018). In his review of the 2021 book, *God save the Queen: The strange persistence of monarchies* by Dennis Altman, McIntyre (2022) observes how the love/hate relationship we have with monarchies unsettles us as much as help us:

> Altman concludes that 'many of us are rational republicans but emotionally attached to the [monarchic] institution in ways that are often embarrassing to acknowledge'. [Altman] sees monarchy as a check on the behaviour of politicians—'a silent brake on the tendency of governments to act authoritatively'. Monarchs stand as buffers to the excesses of authoritarian populists. Historic royal ceremonial provides a sense of continuity and fosters peoples' emotional attachment.
>
> (McIntyre, 2022: 27)

Continuity of and attachment to what exactly? I imagine it is political continuity (democracy?) and an attachment of a socially cohesive nature. Getting a nation united is a relatively easy thing to do when all that is required is a common enemy; an 'us' and 'them' of sorts. What is meant by 'sense of continuity' brings forth ideas of tradition and ways of going about things. Neither aspect is value neutral. We could therefore say for instance, that to embrace academic systems of hierarchies, as ability grouping, provides a sense of continuity *to that system* and fosters children's emotional attachment *to their particular circumstances*. This sense of continuity is enacted in what we perceive as common-sense practices; practices that allow us to feel at home so to speak, on familiar ground. The point however is that we also need to acknowledge that intellectual hierarchies, like ability grouping, reproduce the 'natural order' of things at the other end too: it provides a sense of continued humiliation to those in the bottom set, and fosters emotional attachment to what is antagonistic to academic achievement.

To explore what constitutes meritocratic, common-sense practices is to acknowledge therefore that these notions thrive within the values and 'natural order' of a monarchic and imperial context. To say 'fundamental *British* values' then, has a certain weight and historical resonance. In fact, few notions other than 'human' are capable of comfortably qualifying the concept of 'values'. How are British values different from Irish, French, or Australian values? What is the word

'British' really doing there, other than making a 'them' and 'us' point, reminding us of our imperial nature?

On knowing one's place and the place of others

I used to say to my trainee teachers that the reason children were grouped by ability in UK schools was due to the country's highly manifest monarchy, which promotes the idea that everyone needs 'to know their place',[4] whereas in France, they sharply did away with that idea altogether. After some general amusement, many of my students are surprised to know that ability grouping practices are not how most other countries organize their education systems. Class seems to be a very British affair in popular culture due to its obvious, visual (surroundings), and auditory (accent) cues, as can be seen (and reified) in famous period-drama productions like Downton Abbey or The Crown. Villains in films often have an upper-class British accent.

In the following comedy sketch by The Two Ronnies (1966), the British class system is succinctly enacted. Man A has an upper-class accent, is tall and thin. Man B is middle class, plump and of average height and accent. Man C is working class, short and with a working-class accent:

Man A: I look down on B because I am upper class.
Man B: I look up to A because he is upper class. But I look down on C because he is lower class.
Man C: I know my place.

(Feldman and Law, 1966)

The reason *Class Sketch* is still entertaining is because the truth it conceals and uncovers resonates with us still. In like fashion, many schools have at least three 'ability' sets: set A, set B, and set C. Although the segregation is intellectual rather than economic, research shows that in state schools most pupils in bottom sets come from disadvantaged backgrounds (Resay, 2017; Francis et al., 2017). We must not forget however, that private schools also operate this segregation system, and often in much more rigid ways, and that although class is, of course, also prevalent in other countries, no one seems to do it as well as the British.

In the International Social Survey Programme in 2012, Britain came among the top countries where children are set by ability (Jerrim,

2015) and where meritocratic factors are seen as essential to societal success (Mijs, 2016). In academic circles however, meritocracy as an ideal has experienced a general decline (Sen, 2000; Crawford, 2010; Souto-Otero, 2010; Allen, 2011), and recent writings have less to say to commend it (Meroe, 2014; Littler, 2017). Nevertheless, the concept still appeals to the general public and is often used to explain away social inequalities and educational institutions' decisions. Its hold on schools' practice is therefore not surprising.

Although class may be less openly public in other countries, its impact on who gets the best education is just as insidious. In the United States, children are 'tracked' in classes according to their academic ability, usually in secondary. However,

> In some schools, tracking begins with kindergarten screening. IQ and early achievement tests designed to measure so-called "ability" determine track placement in the elementary years, thus setting in place an educational trajectory for 12 years of schooling.
>
> (Burris and Garrity, 2008: par2)

Some practices in the United States go unethically further still in their embracement of 'corporate culture' and neoliberalist (imperial) agendas, 'some privately-run prison systems in the state carefully monitored the third grade (age 10–11) test scores of male students of colour to predict future prison populations' (Stahl, 2020: 890). Immerwahr (2019) is right to remind us of the emperor's new clothes in the United States: globalization, where many of the old imperial core values find a new home with fertile ground.

As I have suggested thus far, meritocracy alone provides a suspect excuse for ability grouping practices. Imperial values around competitiveness, growth, and class are too compromised with it to be ignored. The economist and philosopher Amartya Sen, notes,

> Merit is underdefined, since it is dependent on the preferred view of a good society. The theory of merit, thus, needs to draw on other normative theories.
>
> (Sen, 2000: 14)

A consequentialist view of education for instance, the idea that all's well that ends well (as well as it can), can make us focus on and praise the great success of the few while making us blind to the injustices suffered by the many. For instance, in Allan Bennett's play, *The history boys*,[5] the light shines on the few 'high ability' boys that make it all the way to Oxford, whereas in Shane Meadows' 2006 film, *This is England*[6] we get an inkling of where some of the 'unacademic', working class boys go in order to feel that sense of belonging. Combo, one of the characters in Meadow's film, joins the National Front where his membership is not only valued but highly sought-after: 'the nation-state has become a passionate site of attachment, a transitional object onto which he can project desire for inclusion and love' (Dyer, 2017: 321), as well as some measure of success and merit. There are no ability notions in patriotism.

If merit was rather seen as the 'credit' of an action, there may be more room for a focus on processes (effort) rather than outcomes, because whereas outcomes can vary, everyone can make the same effort. Effort then is inclusive in its nature but difficult to measure. To say that we didn't succeed academically due to lack of effort frees us from the indignity of a perceived intellectually inferiority, for we can always argue that *had* we put in the effort and applied ourselves we could have merited success (or so we are led to believe). But what is the nature of this merit?

Mark Tapley, a character from Charles Dickens novel Martin Chuzzlewitt (1844), only sees the merit of something where credit is due. For him, success and merit are not measured by any intellectual (or social) outcomes necessarily, but on the cunning exercise of the processes involved. That is to say, for instance, there is credit in smiling only when our heart is broken, for any happy heart may smile. Likewise, there is credit in saying something clever, only if you have not been formally educated, for any educated person may say a clever thing (and many do). Seen this way, crediting success takes account of someone's journey and quiet effort in ways that meritocracy or even value-added measures cannot. Institutions of knowledge are blind to this view of merit. Mr. Tapley's intelligence goes unnoticed by those who consider themselves socially 'above him'. The egocentric character in Pygmalion (Shaw, 1913), Professor Higgins, seems open enough to acknowledge what he describes as 'the natural gift of rhetoric' in Mr. Doolittle (Eliza's working-class father in Pygmalion, or 'My Fair Lady'[7]), who in turn declares himself to belong to the 'undeserving poor, up against middle-class morality', in other words, too poor to afford the luxuries of morals (an example of 'Man C' earlier). Impressed by Mr. Doolittle's rhetoric, Professor Higgins

Meritocracy and its allegiance to the empire 57

recommends him as a key speaker at a Workman's Union event. We could see this as an example of a time when, according to Young's novel, intelligence was still aplenty in the working classes. Academic selection at school had not yet started to cream off such children and placed them in an elite,

> Amongst children who left school for manual jobs in the 1940s one in twenty still had I.Q.s over 120 ... by the last quarter of the century, the supply of really capable working men to fill the top union posts had dried up completely.
>
> (Young, 1994: 135)

Both Mr. Tapley and Mr. Doolittle are examples of the 'one in twenty' who now, in these days, would most probably be placed in the 'high ability' groups during school, destined for higher education.

But, you might say, do we want a nation led by effort rather than intelligence? Michael Young played with such ideas in his dystopian fantasy. What would a society look like if it favoured collaboration over competitiveness and effort over achievement? I imagine it will depend on what is meant by progress; on the sort of progress that we want. As children of the empire, our views on this have already been mapped out. Young observed how what defines us is always contingent upon current values,

> There has never been such gross over-simplification as in modern Britain. Since the country is dedicated to the one overriding purpose of economic expansion, people are judged according to the single test of how much they increase production, or the knowledge that will, directly or indirectly, lead to that consummation.
>
> (Young, 1994: 157)

As adults, we may think the empire is a thing of the past; that we no longer need to 'know our place' within its hierarchies, but we are very quick to make children know their place among their peers. These, unarticulated experiences do not go unnoticed in the child-as-subject—for the child is certainly not a citizen yet; they are subjects of adult scrutiny and literal manipulation: rounded up according to their intellectual abilities. Thus, meritocratic practices help the empire sustain the necessary hierarchies that allow it to function.

Hierarchies of shame

There is something humanly objectionable about the 'sociospatial practice' (Bunnell et al., 2012) of physically placing someone's body in a space that signals their 'inferior' academic ability; about being, without consent, visually categorized by ability (or religion/race) for the contemplation of others. Children in 'low ability' groups feel daily degradation in front of their peers, who are themselves placed as their 'intellectual betters'. Children in 'high ability' groups do not need to do anything to make others feel the humiliation. It is the practice itself that reinforces the shame. Reflecting on what the concept of shame can mean, the moral philosopher, Bernard Williams, observed,

> The basic experience connected with shame is that of being seen, inappropriately, by the wrong people, in the wrong condition. ... The reaction is to cover oneself or to hide, and people naturally take steps to avoid the situations that call for it.
> (Williams, 2008: 78)

Except that children cannot avoid a situation engineered by adults, unless they rebel against it, or escape it relatively. In Frances et al.'s interviews, many children expressed the,

> Shame and anxiety experienced in inhabiting the 'pathologised space' (Reay, 2017) of the bottom set. Unsurprisingly, pupils, particularly those closest to the bottom set, expressed their relief that they had (for now) avoided or escaped being allocated to the most-disparaged grouping:
> *Well, I used to be in Set 5, then I moved up to Set 4, so I'm happy now, because I've moved up. Set 4 is one of the better classes to be in.*
> (Frances et al., 2019: 76)

This relativizes the shame, placing it in a seemingly absurd (to adults) hierarchical system. Another child says,

> *Because I'm in Set 4 I feel a bit embarrassed about that because other people are in the higher sets.*
> (ibid.: 75)

While another redirects attention to better circumstances,

> *For maths I'm in the bottom set and it was hard for me to tell my mum because I thought she'd be disappointed. But because in English I'm in Set 2 my mum is proud of me, like really proud, and I was proud saying it.*
>
> (ibid.: 75)

Many children experience bottom sets for both and more subjects. Some of those lucky enough to be in higher sets may reflect on the predicament of their peers or perhaps simply project their own fears onto them, suggesting that those children probably feel,

> *a bit deflated, like they might wake up and they might not want to go to school because they might be in the bottom set and they just like don't want to go.*
>
> (Frances et al., 2019: 76)

Not engaging with academic work would thus make sense for children who wish to avoid further shame and who have no alternative options (effort was not enough). To say, 'I would succeed if I tried or cared' is to avoid, 'I cared and tried but failed'. The latter has personal implications regarding one's academic identity and self-esteem, which the child, in his or her immaturity cannot properly articulate or address. Williams notes,

> In the experience of shame, one's whole being seems diminished or lessened. In my experience of shame, the other sees all of me and all through me, even if the occasion of the shame is on my surface— for instance, in my appearance; and the expression of shame, in general as well as in the particular form of it that is embarrassment, it's not just a desire to hide, or to hide my face, but the desire to disappear, not to be there. It is not even the wish, as people say, to sink through the floor, but rather the wish that the space occupied by me should be instantaneously empty.
>
> (Williams, 2008: 89)

Of course, the shame that Bernard Williams refers to can be occasioned by many things in one's life, and although his writing here refers to the trials and tribulations of ancient Greek characters (e.g. Odysseus), we can see how children's journey through the school experience is a place of such trials. Children, like Odysseus, face the journey alone, without their parents. If parents were allowed to walk by their side all day at school, I do not believe ability grouping practices would take hold so easily. Parents would not be happy to be themselves grouped according to their child's academic ability. The school odyssey is the child's alone; made up of spaces of happiness or pride, misery or shame.

Concluding thoughts

To conclude with allusions to Homer's Odyssey when considering the role of meritocracy within the values of empire is quite fitting. It speaks to the survival of the fittest; to the way we respond to the whim of the gods (adults) under whose care or indifference we are placed; to the fact that there is a great deal of concealed luck in the concept of meritocracy; that the stage is anything but a fair playing field. Children that spent most of their education in 'lower ability' groups will be too weary to exercise their citizenry conscientiously in adulthood.

Notes

1 Introduced by the Conservative party in 2014, 'promoting British values in schools to ensure young people leave school prepared for life in modern Britain' UK Gov., 2014. The said values are: democracy, rule of law, respect & tolerance, and individual liberty. See Lander (2016).
2 An attempt was made in 2004 by the House of Commons to replace the word Empire with Excellence, but the attempt seems to have got nowhere.
3 John 12:7–8.
4 There is a brief sketch by The Two Ronnies which puts this rather succinctly, www.youtube.com/watch?v=ppv97S3ih14
5 A play (and movie) by Allan Bennett, whose main characters are clever students who succeed academically.
6 A 2006 film by Shane Meadows, based on skinheads' subcultures (depicted as academic failures) in 1983.
7 My Fair Lady is based on Bernard Shaw's play, Pygmalion (1913).

References

Allen, A. (2011). Michael Young's the rise of the meritocracy: A philosophical critique. *British Journal of Educational Studies*, 59(4), 367–382.

Bryson, M. (2004). 'His Tyranny Who Reigns': The Biblical Roots of Divine Kingship and Milton's Rejection of 'Heav'n's King'. *Milton Studies, 43,* 111–144.

Bunnell, T., Yea, S., Peake, L., Skelton, T., & Smith, M. (2012). Geographies of friendships. *Progress in Human Geography, 36*(4), 490–507.

Burris, C. C., & Garrity, D. T. (2008). *Detracking for excellence and equity*. ASCD.

Crawford, C. E. (2017). Promoting 'fundamental British values' in schools: A critical race perspective. *Curriculum Perspectives, 37*(2), 197–204.

Crawford, K. (2010). Schooling, citizenship and the myth of the meritocracy. *Citizenship, Social and Economics Education, 9*(1), 3–13.

Cruz-Medina, J. P. (2018). Between the image of the God and the image of the King: Evangelism and formation of the social body at a Pueblo de Indios of the Kingdom of the New Granada (16th–18th centuries). *Libros de la corte, 17,* 33–51. https://doi.org/10.15366/ldc2018.10.17.002

Dickens, C. (1844). *The life and adventures of Martin Chuzzlewit by Charles Dickens. With illustrations by Phiz*. Chapman and Hall.

Dyer, H. (2017). Reparation for a violent boyhood: Pedagogies of mourning in Shane Meadow's *This is England*. *Pedagogy, Culture & Society, 25*(3), 315–325.

Feldman, M., & Law, J. (Directors). (1966). *Class Sketch II*. BBC1.

Foucault, M. (1979). *Discipline and punish: The birth of the prison; translated from the French by Alan Sheridan*. Vintage Books.

Francis, B., Taylor, B., Tereshchenko, A., Taylor, B., & Tereshchenko, A. (2019). *Reassessing 'ability' grouping: Improving practice for equity and attainment*. Routledge.

Francis, R., Connolly, P., Archer, L., Hodgen, J., Mazenod, A., Pepper, D., Sloan, S., Taylor, B., Tereschchenko, A., & Travers, M. (2017). Attainment grouping as self-fulfilling prophesy? A mixed methods exploration of self-confidence and set level among year 7 students. *International Journal of Educational Research, 86,* 96–108.

Immerwahr, D. (2019). *How to hide an empire: A short history of the greater United States*. Bodley Head.

Jarausch, K. H. (2013). The conundrum of complicity: German professionals and the final solution. In A. E. Steinweis & R. D. Rachlin (Eds.), *The law in Nazi Germany* (1st ed., pp. 15–35). Berghahn Books.

Jerrim, J. (2015). Why do East Asian children perform so well in PISA? An investigation of Western-born children of East Asian descent. *Oxford Review of Education, 41*(3), 310–333.

Kumashiro, K. K. (2015). *Against common sense: Teaching and learning toward social justice* (3rd ed.). Routledge.

Lander, V. (2016). Introduction to fundamental British values. *Journal of Education for Teaching, 42*(3), 274–279. https://doi.org/10.1080/02607476.2016.1184459

Littler, J. (2017). *Against meritocracy: Culture, power and myths of mobility*. Routledge/Taylor & Francis Group.

McIntyre, W. D. (2022). GOD SAVE THE QUEEN: The strange persistence of monarchies. *New Zealand International Review*, *47*(3), 26–28.

Meroe, A. S. (2014). Democracy, meritocracy and the uses of education. *The Journal of Negro Education*, *83*(4), 485.

Mijs, J. J. B. (2016). The unfulfillable promise of meritocracy: Three lessons and their implications for justice in education. *Social Justice Research*, *29*(1), 14–34.

Minerd, M. K. (2018). Intelligence and morality: Translation and comments on an article by Ambroise Gardeil, O.P. *Nova et Vetera*, *16*(2), 643–664.

Prasch, R. E. (2005). Neoliberalism and empire: How are they related? *Review of Radical Political Economics*, *37*(3), 281–287.

Reay, D. (2017). *Miseducation: Inequality, education and the working classes* (1st ed.). Policy Press. https://doi.org/10.2307/j.ctt22p7k7m

Sen, A. (2000). Merit and justice. In K. Arrow, S. Bowles, & S. Durlauf (Eds.), *Meritocracy and economic inequality* (pp. 5–16). Princeton University Press.

Shaw, G. B. (1913). Pygmalion. https://en.wikipedia.org/w/index.php?title=Pygmalion_(play)&oldid=1167169723

Shlaim, A. (2021). *On British colonialism, antisemitism, and Palestinian rights* [News]. Middle East Eye. www.middleeasteye.net/big-story/uk-palestine-israel-policy-balfour-johnson-anitsemitism-colonialism

Sokhi-Bulley, B. (2014, December 2). *Governmentality: Notes on the thought of Michel Foucault*. Critical Legal Thinking.

Souto-Otero, M. (2010). Education, meritocracy and redistribution. *Journal of Education Policy*, *25*(3), 397–413.

Stahl, G. D. (2020). Corporate practices and ethical tensions: Researching social justice values and neoliberal paradoxes in a 'no excuses' charter school. *British Educational Research Journal*, *46*(4), 878–893.

Wafawanaka, R. (2014). Is the biblical perspective on poverty that "there shall be no poor among you" or "you will always have the poor with you"? *Review and Expositor (Berne)*, *111*(2), 107–120.

Wilkins, C. (2011). Professionalism and the post-performative teacher: New teachers reflect on autonomy and accountability in the English school system. *Professional Development in Education*, *37*(3), 389–409.

Williams, B. (2008). *Shame and necessity* (Reprint 2019). University of California Press. https://doi.org/10.1525/9780520934931

Young, M. (1994). *The rise of the meritocracy* (2nd ed.). Transaction Publishers.

Young, T. (2020). The Rise of the Genotocracy. *The Political Quarterly*, *91*(2), 388–396. https://doi.org/10.1111/1467-923X.12831

4 Knowledge and humiliation in schools

Teachers, knowledge, and children

Teacher, knowledge, and children should not be thought of as three separable concepts. To explore each in isolation is to miss two-thirds of a story. When considering the place of philosophy in childhood studies Priscilla Alderson asks, 'Does a "focus on children", partly isolating them from the complex society they share with adults, provide misleading findings? Does it possibly inadvertently reinforce the social exclusion of children?' (Alderson, 2016: 201). A child's school experiences cannot be extricated from what makes that experience what it is. Although it serves an academic purpose to acknowledge the components of the experience, we need to keep their interconnectedness at the fore of our argument. This is why in initial teacher education we speak of 'learning and teaching' and not just teaching. For example, a teacher may think he taught children about the water cycle, while a child may say, when asked, that what she learned was about the oceans. What we intend to teach is not necessarily what children ultimately learn in any given lesson (Shulman, 2004; Biesta, 2010). The child and the teacher are in a constant exchange of moving perspectives. We may call these perspectives knowledge, the truth of which constantly evolves as we mature. These perspectives are not to be confused with relativism. I speak of a human-specific perspective, not an individual's. Thus, whereas personal experience can make children think (know) that the sun orbits the Earth, their acquisition of further, more intellectually mature perspectives (usually abstract) will allow them to know that it is in fact the other way around, contradicting their personal experience. Science often gives us new perspectives that appear to contradict manifest experience. In this sense, perspective allows us to

DOI: 10.4324/9781003398202-5

see the dynamic and situated nature of knowledge. With every lesson, the teacher gets to know a little bit more about the children's immature perspectives, acting accordingly, while children get to know about the teacher's intellectually matured perspective, modifying their own accordingly. It can also allow us to see how each of us 'knows differently' from our own cultural and physically situated paradigm. Our understanding and reach of our physical surroundings are predicated on the perspective set by our height, vision, and mobility; what we have been taught to pay attention to or ignore. Thus, we may have been in the same lesson with others, but we understood, remembered, or internalized the contents differently. In this sense, knowledge is not just information. Information is what we find in textbooks or on the Internet (seemingly endless); information gets passed on from perspective to perspective, and in the process, it gets augmented, changed, concealed, distorted, distributed, etc. Information and perspective offer us the paradigm of knowledge; how we have managed to make sense of that information as part of a particular repertoire of perspectives and expressions. So, we can appreciate how knowledge cannot be separate from what it means to be a 'child' or a 'teacher' and is therefore incommensurable and non-quantifiable. Information, on the other hand, is easy to measure, and it is often what the business of school entails. Reducing knowledge to the acquisition of information does not promote a cultivation of thinking. As a rule of thumb, whatever a computer does, is an information-based process, however complex it may be. Only the human can deal in knowledge, for the inferential nature of language is underpinned by our need to know *why* things happen (Brandom, 1994; Surendran, 2023).

We may be very familiar with children's *why* questions, and if we were lucky as children, we will have been indulged and continue learning about the world in that way. Most schooling however, puts a swift stop to children's innate curiosity, leading Sir Ken Robinson (2015) to observe that most children are 'educated out' of their creativity while in school. Most schools seem to deal exclusively with information. As discussed in the previous chapter, empires (the so called 'neo-liberal' states) have great investment in the accumulation of information that can lead to further knowledge and power. Schools speak of knowledge when in fact, they mostly mean information, thus applying the language of the latter to aspects of the former, making knowledge appear quantifiable, as if one could in fact distribute or confer knowledge on others. *Knowledge* in schools, however, is usually left to the few children at the top, while *information* is the bread of the rest, particularly so for the supposedly 'low ability' children. If we speak of knowledge rather than information, what sort of knowledge is a child acquiring in school? How do we learn, for instance, that some information is important, dismissible, laughable, or essential? These qualifiers usually form part of our knowledge base, and as teachers we implicitly enact these qualifiers, these perspectives and values on a given set of information, which then children implicitly learn. Our attitudes and values are the processors and gatekeepers of all incoming and outgoing information, shaping our knowledge base (and our children's propensities) accordingly. Teachers need to be aware of their own attitudes and values.

To explore this further, a distinction needs to be made between curriculum content and its delivery. The former is usually set by governments and not by teachers or school. To challenge the values inherent in a curriculum is a systemic, structural challenge. In contrast, a teacher's attitudes and values are most likely manifest *during* his teaching, which I will here forth refer to as the *delivery* of the lesson plan, and the school's values are mostly manifest in its *organization* of teaching and learning. Both the delivery and the organization are always performative acts, more readily accessible challenges at the ground level. The *delivery* of a lesson can reveal our values because in it we are placed in the moment: in the midst of an act. Children learn values (which qualify our world) from adults' attitudes and actions rather than from adults' words. Thus, a teacher (or any of us) may never be aware of the effect of his actions or habits. The political philosopher, Hannah Arendt (1958), makes a useful distinction between action and making that reflects this difference (Donne, 1997). An educational example of each is the *delivery* of a lesson (the action) and the *lesson plan* (the making). The lesson plan includes the content, resources, and sequence of presentation, but it can also (it should) include aspects of delivery, for example, how we phrase something, the classroom layout, timings, and children's movements. However, regardless of how thorough a lesson plan is, the delivery is always something contingent on the moment and on who is enacting it and with whom. Action involves the unpredictable flux of speech, action, and reaction, from others and from what happens and back again. In a teacher's case, this works in a context of impressionable, vulnerable others, incipient acquirers of our norms and values. For Arendt, in action, men disclose themselves as subjects, ... unique persons, even when they wholly concentrate upon reaching an altogether worldly, material object.

(Arendt, 1958: 183)

She adds,

He who acts never quite knows what he is doing, ... he always becomes 'guilty' of consequences he never intended or even foresaw [and] can never undo.

(Arendt, 1958: 233)

It is in the delivery of lessons then, that our attitudes, values, and perspectives on education come implicitly to the fore, often unbeknown to us. Being aware of this can at least put us on guard as to certain attitudes we may never have questioned before (shoulder shrugs, rolling of eyes, dismissive phrases, etc.). A teacher who engages in ability grouping practices is already on dangerous ground, passing on to children an important lesson about who 'can learn' and who 'cannot learn', which is an attitude towards being and knowledge.

Epistemic injustice: thoughts on Miranda Fricker

We are familiar with terms such as 'social injustice' which happens when a society is structured in ways that markedly marginalize or deprive members of particular groups from opportunities for improvement, for instance, lack of access to basic education. Epistemic injustice, meaning injustices that are caused by denying knowledge or ways of knowing to those others, can also marginalize and deprive them of opportunities. These injustices are not easy to see because they sit in people's perspectives rather than circumstances, for instance, interacting with children in minimal ways, thus excluding them from critical thinking on certain topics and from the use of more elaborate vocabulary, denying or lowering their level of access to more demanding material. These acts may adversely impact not only their chances of entry to college, but more critically, the effective articulation of social injustices they might suffer. The concept of epistemic injustice was developed by Miranda Fricker (2007) to unpick relations of social power pertaining to knowledge. Fricker defines social power as, a practically socially situated capacity to control others' actions, where this capacity may be exercised (actively or passively) by particular social agents, or alternatively, it may operate purely structurally.

(Fricker, 2007: 14)

There are further distinctions that Fricker makes in terms of epistemic injustice that are relevant here, and which I will exemplify through the school context.

Testimonial injustice refers to someone's testimony; what they declare to know. It is an injustice that takes place between the hearer (an individual or a system) and the speaker. It is to declare from a perspective of prejudice (including unconscious prejudices) that what someone 'speaks' is not valid, credible nor adequate (Nutbrown, 2016). For instance, dismissing a child's account of an incident as insufficient, confused, or incorrect, on the grounds that he is a child as well as on account of him being in a 'low ability' group. When a (brave) child says that she does not deserve to be placed in a 'low ability' group or class, teachers deny credibility to that statement. They may listen but are unlikely to act. The child becomes the content she spoke, what she wrote, what she remembered, but not a person attempting to escape humiliation.

The injustice or moral objection to ability grouping is threefold:

a it is a form of hierarchical segregation that cuts to the core of our individual identity and self-esteem;
b people should be free of unwarranted and avoidable humiliating practices, and,
c the cumulative effects of this type of segregation narrows the horizons of thought of an individual, negatively impacting their future relation with organized forms of knowledge.

How educational systems are organized as well as the curriculum content they offer, form part of the organizational structure of the school. To think of an injustice as *structural*, means that it is not teachers necessarily who are directly at fault (the transactional agents), but the educational institutions within which they work and whose logic they enact. Segregating children by ability, would thus constitute a *structural testimonial* injustice, implicating the school system as perpetrator, with teachers as its immediate, perceived transactional agents, and the children, whose words were unable to testify 'adequately', as the recipients of the injustice; the 'have-nots' of information (children in 'low ability' groups).

There is another type of injustice that school children, in their immaturity, are particularly vulnerable to. Not yet having reached their full linguistic capacity, children can lack the language of expression that can help them articulate a given injustice. Fricker (2007) called this kind of epistemic injustice, a *hermeneutic injustice*. For instance, children can feel humiliation even if they don't yet know the word 'humiliation'. Being moved to the 'low ability' table or to the bottom set class is a humiliating event that children may not be able to articulate and therefore, cannot complain about. But even if children have acquired the language to articulate their plight, it is doubtful that they will use it in explicit and effective resistance due to the dynamics of power relations and their lack of understanding of the norms governing adult behaviour towards them. A university student who is placed in a 'low ability' table will rightly complain, even if the university argues it is for his own good. Universities do not inflict this type of injustice on 'paying customers' who have the power and linguistic acumen to complain and sue.

For children in the bottom sets, there is a cross-sectional and intergenerational injustice (Murris, 2013) taking place as well. When the child is literally, physically put 'in his or her place' and inducted through the entirety of their school life into a system of 'low ability' or 'bottom set' citizenry, his parents and the child's own descendants (or followers) may be partaking of the injustice. Some minority ethnic groups, for instance, who have been relegated to 'low ability' tables and subsequently to 'bottom sets', leave school with an even stronger sense of *not* belonging to the oppressive, national identity of the majority, and hold on steadfastly instead to the unconditional acceptance that their own communities bestow (Derrington and Kendall, 2004; Devine and McGillicuddy, 2019).

Assessment as means to humiliation

The conflation of knowledge with information has muddled our understanding of what knowledge means and entails, and hence, on what it is that we are actually assessing children, whether summative or formatively. Miranda Fricker defines epistemic injustice as, 'a wrong done to someone specifically in their capacity as a knower'

Knowledge and humiliation in schools 69

(Fricker, 2007: 1). The conceptualization of 'children as knowers' in a social context of inferential learning following Vygotsky (1978) and Brandom (1994) allows us to see children as beings who are 'capable of *judgment*, rather than of merely mechanical responses to stimuli' (Derry, 2006: par11). However, 'mechanical responses to stimuli' is usually the kind of 'knowing' that is assessed at school, and on which children are visibly categorized as 'knowers'. Schools work rather on a narrow view of children as knowers, focusing instead on their memory for facts and their skills in language and number.

How much one knows is often seen as a question of how much one remembers. Writing skills, for instance, are seldom based on the child as an individual reflexive being (Ryan, 2014). Also, teachers' perspectives on assessment seldom include cultural awareness in terms of a responsiveness to children's varied backgrounds (Walters, 2007; Vass, 2015; Nortvedt, 2020). In the school context of assessment, for instance, 'to know' division or binomial equations is to remember the time tables and a process; 'to know' about materials is to remember a system of representational classification; 'to know' what a 'good' sentence is, is to remember to use a verb, plus adjectives and adverbs generously (grades often reflect form over content); and 'to know' what *me gusta ir a la playa* means is to remember a translation. Many secondary students memorize a whole chunk of foreign text for their exams, not always knowing what it means.

Although instrumental (formulaic or rote) learning in itself is not knowledge, this is the kind of learning that usually gets assessed either through a grade or through teacher observation. Children are thus placed in an 'instrumental knowledge' hierarchy, that is to say, an information hierarchy of a descriptive nature, e.g. how well, according to prescribed patterns and connections, they can describe, explain, or exemplify something. In this way, the assessment of instrumental knowledge that leads to ability grouping practices splits the class (or the school) between the 'haves and have-nots' of instrumental knowledge.

> [W]hen we did our end of year assessments, Set 1 and Set 2 got different papers which were a lot harder than ours, but then Set 3, Set 4, Set 5, and Set 6 would, like, get the same paper which will make us feel dumb because, like, someone's smart but like they've got to do the dumb, lower paper, because of their set.
> (Set 3 English and Maths boy, in Francis et al., 2019: 75)

Francis et al. comment how this boy's words, 'evoke embarrassed frustration, hierarchisation, and the equation of being in a low set with being "dumb"' (ibid.: 75). Little has changed in almost 20 years, for I remember the children in my bottom set French class referring to themselves in those exact terms. The extensive research conducted by Francis et al. also threw light on how children in middle and top sets construct the plight of their 'humiliated' peers in terms of school becoming a place you might not want to wake up for.

Humiliation, one of the most cognitively demanding emotions (Otten and Jonas, 2013) has been described as containing mostly emotions of

> feeling powerless, small, and inferior in a situation in which one is brought down and in which an audience is present—which may contribute to these diminutive feelings—leading the person to appraise the situation as unfair and resulting in a mix of emotions, most notably disappointment, anger, and shame.
> (Elshout et al., 2017: 1592)

This is aptly qualified by emphasizing the social nature of humiliation which may account for its greater cognitive intensity, because it is a 'complex social emotion that involves monitoring loss of social status' (Jarrett, 2014). Laing (2023) quotes Nussbaum's more cautious thoughts which assert that, 'humiliation typically makes the statement that the person in question is low, not on a part with others in terms of human dignity' (Nussbaum, 2004: 204, in Laing, 2023: 7).

Legette's research in the United States shows the same stigmatization of children (particularly black children) tracked in non-honours classes. He recalls one such participant, observing that, 'she and her classmates were told several times by students in honours that "You're dumb cause, you can't read, so you in the slow class"' (Legette, 2018: 1318). Legette confirms how children thus acquire their academic identities through their school experience. A boy in the study observes,

> I really don't know why they have us in these classes like they do, but I know the test we take has something to do with it. I guess if we were smarter with better scores we would be in a different class but we not, we need more help, I guess.
> (Legette, 2018: 1318)

In Australian studies similar findings are noted, where meritocratic practices marginalize First Nations children by labelling their efforts as poor or insufficient; practices that are inattentive to historical injustices and dismissive of racist prejudices (Vass, 2015). Other studies observe how students deemed 'high ability' can thus internalize the meritocratic principles of 'just-deserts', in often cruel ways,

> I prefer to be in the higher class because you don't get interrupted all the time by all the idiots. There are not as many idiots in it [i.e. the higher-stream classroom] that muck around all the time.
> (Zevenbergen, 2005: 615)

Children in bottom sets (or lower streams) have to cope not only with the stigma attached to their 'station', but also with the knowledge that the education they receive has a reduced content and is therefore assessed differently, in plain sight,

> In our class we only cover the core content, so I can only do questions 1 and 2 on the exam. The others I don't know how to do as we have not done them in class. These are the questions that get you higher marks and we can't do them. So the most I can get on the exam is a pass. (Beechwood, Year 10; lower stream)
> (in Zevenbergen, 2005: 614)

When we speak of assessment then, we refer not only to the fact that children are assessed in terms of what they supposedly 'know', failing to reach a required benchmark, but that the assessment itself limits the possibility of reaching that benchmark; the possibility of escape from the bottom sets.

The kind of instrumental knowledge favoured in schools, both propositional (knowing that) and procedural (knowing how) are often reduced to their most basic forms of assessment (multiple choice, matching tasks, gap-filling, copying, etc.), particularly for 'low ability' groups/classes (Wilson, 2011; Ryan, 2014; Blatchford and Webster, 2018). This encourages children to think about knowledge in those reduced terms. Failing assessment can thus be seen as a failure 'as a knower'; a personal event that carries material consequences and exposes them to humiliation. For the children in the bottom sets, assessment and knowledge become linked in a despairing dance whose rhythm is impossible to inhabit. The wonder and curiosity they may once have had is thus nipped in the bud. Such a warped received view of knowledge turns it into the direct means to their humiliation. It seems logical then to ask why such children should trust knowledge that has been used to humiliate them. Why value its power to explain anything, e.g. climate change, health, or the roundness of the earth? Why value different cultures or foreign sounds? Such children are robbed of trust towards certain types of formalized knowledge; deprived of the privileged status of a top (or middle) set student, and thus, discouraged from acquiring a desire to follow avenues of knowledge in the particular areas where they felt discredited or disqualified. When children from disadvantaged backgrounds are in 'low ability' groups/classes throughout most of their school life, they internalize their identity as in opposition to epistemic virtue. The humiliation experienced encourages them to find acceptance and a sense of worth elsewhere, away from notions of truth and knowledge that require intellectual effort and engagement. Having suffered humiliation at the hands of an institution of knowledge, bottom set children are indirectly taught to mistrust and reject such institutions and their speakers. When academic knowledge is weaponized by being used as the means of one's humiliation, the relationship between child and academic knowledge is warped.

Structural injustices need structural responses: notes on Elizabeth Anderson

The 'gaze of the empire', discussed in the previous chapter, can help us explore the sources of some injustices, in terms of whether they are of a transactional or structural nature. The gaze of the empire (the Western values and standards the West holds, defends and spreads worldwide) is enacted through each individual sympathizer. In terms of education, this makes each lecturer, tutor, teacher, and teacher assistant, the empire's finer *channels of power* in Foucauldian terms. In this way, individual transactions (the judgment or action of one person over another) have their roots in a structural entity. Decisions made at governmental level and which educational institutions must adhere to are of a structural nature; bigger than any one individual. Likewise, the values we uphold as a society are structurally passed on, i.e. we are taught, directly or indirectly, to believe in democracy, meritocracy, etc. Values, however, even though they have structural foundations, *feel* very personal, and although the reasons for grouping children by ability have structural and social bases, in the eyes of the child, assessment may appear to be a *transactional injustice*, meaning coming directly from an individual (the teacher). The moment a child experiences the same injustice at the hands of different teachers, across time, then he or she may realize that resistance is indeed futile. Consider the comment from this child in a set 4 Maths class,

> I've heard people, they like freak out about being moved down a set and then they even get jealous if people get moved up. It's like, 'Don't worry about it. Just get used to it'.
> (in Francis et al., 2019: 81)

Compliance is the most immediate way of surviving a structural injustice, and if you are a child, it is often and ultimately the only way. *How* children comply is another matter. In her reply to Miranda Fricker, Elizabeth Anderson (2012) disagrees with the notion that structural injustices can be dealt by single individuals. Yes, a teacher or a school may decide *not* to group children by ability, but a different teacher or a new Principal can undo this. Personal values feel as though they have an impact, but this impact is usually local and vulnerable to be superseded by someone else's values, particularly the majority's values. In Anderson's view, structural injustices demand structural responses. Ethnocentrism, for instance (the 'imperial gaze') of the majority in western and English-speaking countries, allows us to dismiss or hold prejudices against certain speakers because they do not fall within markers of credibility, an act which constitutes an epistemic injustice. Although ethnocentrism refers specifically to the dominance of one culture's gaze over the culture of another, I extend its reach inwards, that is to say, the dominance of the gaze of the powerful over those without power, within the same ethnic environment. Children in different sets or 'ability' groups, acquire, as the excerpts above show, a distinct group identity, for better or for worse. Anderson says,

> If the different groups engaged in inquiry are segregated along lines of salient social identities that are also the basis of systematic unjust group inequalities, then ethnocentrism will cause the advantaged groups to discount the testimony of disadvantaged groups. This will reinforce the epistemic disadvantages of the latter groups and

damage the epistemic standing of their members. Ethnocentrism thereby causes a form a structural testimonial injustice.

(Anderson, 2012: 170)

Some ethnic minorities are overrepresented in bottom sets. Within academic discourse and educational contexts, this ethnocentric, imperial gaze, has definite standards and clear markers of credibility, for instance, markers we call 'academic standards'. Usually, the more 'rigorous' their application the higher the epistemic status of the speaker, and the greater the chances of their testimony being taken seriously (i.e. published) by 'reputable' institutions of knowledge. This is perhaps as it should be. The problem lies in the way children are encouraged (or discouraged) to participate in the process from a young age because of the label placed upon them. The issue is that the imperial gaze, in its fascination for hierarchy, accumulation, competition, and growth, works even against its own people. Academic standards (the assessment of knowledge) is thus a weapon that serves to cut off, deny access and credibility to those whose testimony, for some reason, is deemed insufficient. This denial might be acceptable if it wasn't accompanied by the act of respective labelling and segregation. It is never acceptable when it leads to lack of opportunities or to full and informed social participation in later life, which ultimately affects us all.

An important observation Anderson makes is the benefits of full participation where different groups merge. This is observable when the different ability groups/classes are momentarily dissolved (for subjects other than Maths, English, foreign languages, or science), allowing children to work together. This allows children in 'low ability' groups access to other children's ways of being, thinking, and behaving.

> When they engage in inquiry together on terms of equality, members of disadvantaged groups can gain epistemic favor in the eyes of the privileged by taking advantage of ethnocentric biases (Gaertner and Dovidio 2000). Shared inquiry also tends to produce a shared reality, which can help overcome hermeneutical injustice and its attendant testimonial injustices. In shorthand, we could say that the virtue of epistemic justice for institutions is otherwise known as epistemic democracy: universal participation on terms of equality of all inquirers.
>
> (Anderson, 2012: 171)

The benefits of such participation, however, are soon eclipsed by the negatively reinforcing impact of ability grouping. Such epistemic democracy does not find the fertile ground that a 'shared reality' offers; a place where we can empathize with others as well as learn how to navigate their contexts, discourse, and standards.

Concluding thoughts

The values in-action of a school can differ from the ones it publicly proclaims to believe in. Many schools, for instance, boast publicly of fostering a 'growth mindset' while engaging, contradictorily, in the practice of ability grouping (Towers, 2019), a practice which, incidentally, is never referred to on schools' websites. If the 'received values' schools hold means they continue to ignore the mounting research evidence *against* ability grouping practices, then the easiest structural change would be for governments to ban the practice altogether on ethical grounds; it is a contravention of article 29.1.a from the Children's Rights, 'the education of the child [not only some children] shall be directed to the development of the child's personality, talents and mental and physical abilities to their *fullest* potential'. Only children in the top set (and this with some caveats) benefit in this sense. However, no one's success, be that an empire or a single individual, is worth the humiliation of others.

We should question if the values that children in the bottom sets learn to acquire—in order to survive that humiliation—can ever be compatible with the school's or with any idea of 'respect and tolerance' that the Fundamental British Values, or any democratic system professes to foster.

References

Alderson, P. (2016). The philosophy of critical realism and childhood studies. *Global Studies of Childhood*, 6(2), 199–210. https://doi.org/10.1177/20436 10616647640

Anderson, E. (2012). Epistemic justice as a virtue of social institutions. *Social Epistemology*, 26(2), 163–173. https://doi.org/10.1080/02691 728.2011.652211

Arendt, H. (1958). *The Human Condition; (Charles R. Walgreen Foundation Lectures)* (3rd Printing). The University of Chicago Press. www.biblio. com/book/human-condition-charles-r-walgreen-foundation/d/1552057966

Biesta, G. J. J. (2010). Why 'what works' still won't work: From evidence-based education to value-based education. *Studies in Philosophy and Education*, *29*(5), 491–503. https://doi.org/10.1007/s11217-010-9191-x

Blatchford, P., & Webster, R. (2018). Classroom contexts for learning at primary and secondary school: Class size, groupings, interactions and special educational needs. *British Educational Research Journal*, *44*(4), 681–703.

Brandom, R. (1994). *Making it explicit: Reasoning, representing & discursive commitment: Reasoning, representing and discursive commitment*. Harvard University Press.

Derrington, C., & Kendall, S. (2004). *Gypsy traveller students in secondary schools: A culture, identity and achievement*. Institute of Education Press (IOE Press). http://ebookcentral.proquest.com/lib/ucl/detail.action?docID=1816042

Derry, J. (2006). What is it to be a human knower? *Philosophy Now*, *63*, 10–11.

Devine, D., & McGillicuddy, D. (2019). Explorations of care and care injustice in the everyday lives of Irish Traveller children. *Gender and Education*, *31*(5), 618–630. https://doi.org/10.1080/09540253.2019.1609653

Dunne, J. (1997). Hannah Arendt's distinction between action and making in the human condition. In *Back to the rough ground*. University of Notre Dame Press.

Elshout, M., Nelissen, R. M. A., & van Beest, I. (2017). Conceptualising humiliation. *Cognition and Emotion*, *31*(8), 1581–1594. https://doi.org/10.1080/02699931.2016.1249462

Francis, B., Taylor, B., Tereshchenko, A., Taylor, B., & Tereshchenko, A. (2019). Reassessing 'Ability' grouping: Improving practice for equity and attainment. Routledge. https://doi.org/10.4324/9780429436512

Fricker, M. (2007). Epistemic injustice: Power and the ethics of knowing. In *Epistemic injustice*. Oxford University Press. https://oxford.universitypressscholarship.com/view/10.1093/acprof:oso/9780198237907.001.0001/acprof-9780198237907

Jarrett, C. (2014). Does this brain research prove that humiliation is the most intense human emotion? *Wired*. www.wired.com/2014/05/does-this-brain-research-prove-that-humiliation-is-the-most-intense-human-emotion/

Laing, J. (2023). The harm of humiliation. *European Journal of Philosophy*. https://doi.org/10.1111/ejop.12879

Legette, K. (2018). School tracking and youth self-perceptions: Implications for academic and racial identity. *Child Development*, *89*(4), 1311–1327. https://doi.org/10.1111/cdev.12748

Murris, K. (2013). The epistemic challenge of hearing child's voice. *Studies in Philosophy and Education*, *32*(3), 245–259. https://doi.org/10.1007/s11217-012-9349-9

Nortvedt, G. A., Wiese, E., Brown, M., Burns, D., McNamara, G., O'Hara, J., Altrichter, H., Fellner, M., Herzog-Punzenberger, B., Nayir, F., & Taneri,

P. O. (2020). Aiding culturally responsive assessment in schools in a globalising world. *Educational Assessment, Evaluation and Accountability*, *32*(1), 5–27. https://doi.org/10.1007/s11092-020-09316-w

Nutbrown, G. (2016). *Trusting teachers within reason: Education and the epistemology of testimony*. UCL University College London.

Otten, M., & Jonas, K. J. (2013). Out of the group, out of control?: The brain responds to social exclusion with changes in cognitive control. *Social Cognitive and Affective Neuroscience*, *8*(7), 789–794. https://doi.org/10.1093/scan/nss071

Robinson, K. (2015). The education system is a dangerous myth. In *The Times Educational Supplement* (Issue 5145). Times Supplements Ltd. https://search.proquest.com/docview/2327742503?pq-origsite=primo

Ryan, M. (2014). Reflexive writers: Re-thinking writing development and assessment in schools. *Assessing Writing*, *22*(October), 60–74. https://doi.org/10.1016/j.asw.2014.08.002

Shulman, L. S. (2004). *The wisdom of practice: Essays on teaching, learning, and learning to teach; edited by Suzanne M. Wilson; foreword by Pat Hutchings*. Jossey-Bass.

Surendran, S. (2023). *Inferentialism and science education: Towards meaningful communication in primary science classrooms*. UCL University College London.

Towers, E., Taylor, B., Tereshchenko, A., & Mazenod, A. (2019). 'The reality is complex': Teachers' and school leaders' accounts and justifications of grouping practices in the English key stage 2 classroom. *Education 3–13*, *48*(1), 22–36. https://doi.org/10.1080/03004279.2019.1569707

Vass, G. (2015). Putting critical race theory to work in Australian education research: 'we are with the garden hose here'. *Australian Educational Researcher*, *42*(3), 371–394. https://doi.org/10.1007/s13384-014-0160-1

Vygotsky, L. S. (1978). *Mind in society: The development of higher psychological processes*. Harvard University Press.

Walters, S. (2007). How do you know that he's bright but lazy? Teachers' assessments of Bangladeshi English as an additional language pupils in two year three classrooms. *Oxford Review of Education*, *33*(1), 87–101. https://doi.org/10.1080/03054980601094644

Wilson, P. (2011). *A rapid evidence assessment: Investigating the drop in attainment during the transition phase with a particular focus on child poverty*. Welsh Assembly Government.

Zevenbergen, R. (2005). The construction of a mathematical habitus: Implications of ability grouping in the middle years. *Journal of Curriculum Studies*, *37*(5), 607–619.

5 When knowledge does not pay

I recall teaching many a bottom set for French and Spanish. As the literature confirms, behaviour in 'low ability' groups or sets is notoriously difficult to manage (Didau, 2016). The good working relationship that a teacher may forge with these students is essential for anyone to learn anything, including the teacher. As Mr. Tapley from the previous chapter might say, anyone can teach or be heard by a captive and willing audience; there is little credit in teaching top sets. The real merit is when a teacher can teach a highly reluctant and difficult audience; children who seem unwilling to be taught or be at school at all. Getting these children to develop a sense of epistemic virtue (to cultivate an appreciation to learn) … Now, there is great credit and merit in that.

When considering the article in Figure 5.1, we must remember that in the United Kingdom, the term 'middle classes' refers to the wealthy and/or professional individuals/families. The aim was to attract middle-class pupils. The head teacher himself had been rejected from a grammar school as a child for failing the entrance exam. The now named, Stationers' Crown Academy in south London, still groups children by ability between the school buildings. The article (Figure 5.1) quoted a girl aged 15,

> There was an argument in the school the other day and the girls were arguing between the fences … it just feels like we've been cut off from them.
>
> (Davis, 2011)

Vygotsky's ZPD: zone of proximal development

Being in proximity (rather than cut off) to those who might help us take the next step in our understanding is the principal idea behind

School colour-codes pupils by ability

A secondary school has divided its students by ability, complete with different uniforms. Innovative way to lure the middle classes, or worrying segregation?

Some pupils at Crown Woods College like the small school model, but not everyone is happy about the overt streaming. Photograph: Graham Turner for the Guardian

Figure 5.1 Three different colour ties to reflect three different abilities.

Source: Davis (2011).

Vygotsky's zone of proximal development (ZPD). In *Mind in society* (1978), Lev Vygotsky catalysed and revolutionized the way we think about children's learning and development. Vygotsky's ideas encompass the social and the psychosocial. For him, all our mental functions, 'such as memory, attention, perception and abstraction [are] inextricably connected to our social being' (Derry, 2006: 3), social beings who navigate their world, in terms of commitments and entitlements, through language (Brandom, 1994). In this way, that a child finds herself placed in a 'low ability' group, is a mode of asking '*why* am I here?'. In her search for *reasons*, she will scrutinize others' behaviours (i.e. teachers, peers, parents, etc.), their words, in relation to her immediate context. The evolving synthesis of this helps the child place herself in the world; in the space of reasons, reinforcing or altering her self-concept and esteem. We articulate our identity and plight to ourselves and others through language, and the ZPD provides the first words within reach,

> what children can do with the assistance of others [which] might be in some sense even more indicative of their mental development than what they can do alone. ... allowing not only for what already has been achieved developmentally but also for what is in the course of maturing.
>
> (Vygotsky, 1978: 87)

In this way, children know about the world through and with others, particularly those others who can demonstrate, directly or indirectly, what the next steps or approaches in any given situation might be. This 'other' has been characterized as 'the most knowledgeable other' (Abtahi et al., 2017) who conscious or unconsciously allows one to reach the next step. Vygotsky sees the larger social context of the child as of fundamental importance, '*human learning presupposes a specific social nature and a process by which children grow into the intellectual life of those around them*' (ibid.: 88). In this context, the most-knowledgeable-other is pivotal to learning.

Unfortunately, the social aspect of childhood is seldom a consideration in ability grouping practices; 'bespoke' and 'personalised' teaching are the dubious and de-socialized reasons one often hears. However, learning, for Vygotsky, entailed not only subject content,

> learning is a necessary and universal aspect of the process of developing culturally organized, specifically human, psychological functions.
>
> (ibid.: 90)

and therefore we must consider what it is that children learn through the way educational systems are organized, as well as what the profile of the most-knowledgeable-other may be in the 'low ability' group context.

Vygotsky emphasized motivation in dialogic thinking; the thinking that always addresses another and is motivated by a sense of internal or external audience,

> In the field of psychology, the law of sociogenesis, as propounded by the French psychologist Pierre Janet may have influenced

Vygotsky's thinking on how individual mental processes originate on the social plane.

(Eun, 2019: 19)

Whenever others are concerned, there will always be an affective element to learning where the most-knowledgeable-other is implicated. Referring to Vygotsky and the affective motivational scaffolding that children are given when solving a cognitive task, Luković (2022) says,

> We must take into account that thought has its origins in the motivating sphere of consciousness, a sphere that includes our inclinations and needs, our interests and impulses, and our affect and emotion. … Vygotsky compares thought to a hovering cloud that gushes a shower of words, and to extend this analogy, he compares the motivation of thought to the wind that puts the cloud in motion.
>
> (102)

What sort of 'direction', then, does ability grouping encourage in children? This 'wind' seems to be another way of articulating the imperial gaze (Chapter 3). Our social norms and values give direction to our thoughts. For instance, in an individualistic, utilitarian society where competition is valued over cooperation, and where social hierarchies are visibly marked, then—and often regardless of what research may say—it can seem logical to group children by ability to maximize academic outcome, as the Stationers' Crown Academy does. The values (rather than information) drive our thoughts and actions. Educational systems will act accordingly. The issue is, of course, that the maximization of academic outcomes is only for those who will be at the top of the hierarchy; the 'top sets', the 'honors', the winners of the 'learning competition' that fit in so well with meritocratic practices.

Examples of how values (the wind) trump information (research) are unwittingly provided by most government documents published offering guidance on children's emotional well-being. These, however, never mention ability grouping practices as being the principal strategy (i.e. National Children's Bureau report by Weare, 2015). Initiatives that are meant to improve children's well-being simply do not listen to research on ability grouping. We cannot *talk* children out of feeling a humiliation; we can only model better ways of being, by banishing the practice altogether. For instance, bringing awareness of child-based risk factors like, 'specific learning difficulties; communication difficulties; academic failure and low self-esteem', the Department for Education (2005: 10), declared that,

> Pupils are unlikely to be able to learn effectively if their basic needs for safety, belonging and self-esteem are not met. Action to address risk and resilience factors, and to meet an individual's basic and higher-level needs, will, in turn, enhance the person's emotional health and well-being. The school is a natural setting for much of this to occur. Positive everyday interactions between a teacher and a vulnerable pupil can develop a more positive view of relationships and build that pupil's emotional resilience.
> (DfE, 2005: 11)

Few schools make the connection between self-esteem and being placed in bottom sets. What is, for instance, a positive everyday interaction between an oppressor and its victim? Almost 20 years later, ability grouping still thrives in most schools, with most of the vulnerable children being allocated to 'low ability' groups, and with 'resilience' being heralded as *the* quality to possess, putting the onus on the child.

And what exactly is meant by 'emotional resilience' and why would this be required in the school context? The Children's Society describes emotional resilience to children as,

> Your ability to respond to stressful or unexpected situations and crises. The amount of emotional resilience you have is determined by a number of different things, including your age, identity and what you've experienced in your life.
> (The Children's Society, 2023)

Do schools ever consider themselves as providing 'stressful or unexpected situations of crisis' that require children to develop resilience? It is the child who decides what is stressful or what constitutes a crisis. Ability grouping is not far off a kind of academic bullying, made worse by it being perpetrated and sanctioned by adults. Schools either refuse to see or spell out the stresses (the moral questions) that the practice inflicts on children. They couldn't. We cannot call out an injustice that we have no intention of stopping. It is akin to giving a first aid kit to someone we habitually harm in the name of, *it's for your own good.*

Reflecting on the political and the moral education of children, Judith Suissa suggests we,

> take such 'moral engagement' into the school itself, and try to engage children in a real understanding of the political realm and political discussion as involving basic moral questions ... As a way into this endeavour, the question '*Are there some things we shouldn't be resilient to?*' has clear echoes of Martin Luther King's idea of 'creative maladjustment'.
>
> (Suissa, 2015: 111, my italics)

Resilience is being used as a type of opium; a numbness that allow us to 'carry on'. Sadly enough, the three resilience strategies that The Children's Society offers children are themselves incoherent and compound the epistemic injustice. These are, 'getting a sense of perspective', 'practicing positivity', and 'giving yourself a break'. How can any of this be possible for a child who experiences indirect humiliation by adults and directly by peers at school? How can anyone feel positive about their humiliation, or take a break from it? How can humiliation be *for* anyone's *own good*?

And yet, children are resilient in ways adults do not care for; the kind of *creative maladjustment* that Suissa recalls in the quote above, may well entail an unexpected change of perspective in the child. To explore the possible strategies children may employ to develop resilience, let us consider how the ZPD and the most-knowledgeable-other might function in the 'low ability' classroom context.

Why am I here? When modelling trumps knowledge

I discussed (Chapter 4) how the act of teaching (the delivery of a lesson) is different from a lesson plan, following Hannah Arendt's distinction between *action* and *making* (Dunne, 1997). But there is a further, more nuanced distinction she makes between *action* and *behaviour*. When we ask a child to 'behave', we have certain already fixed notions on what 'behave' means in 'statistical' ways that conform to a norm. Dunne comments,

> 'Action', in this sense, is to be distinguished from 'behavior', which is the activity that can be reliably expected from people who have forfeited their distinctiveness to all-consuming sameness of

'society'. It is an unfortunate truth, in Arendt's view, that the more people there are, the more likely they are to behave and the less likely to tolerate non-behavior.

(1997: 89)

Children learn how to behave in school, in the classroom, in the playground, etc., learning to participate in expected, context-dependent ways. As such, adults can behave 'as teachers' while in school, which is a public sphere. Action (including speech), in Arendt's terms, although also a public act, is one which is less under our conscious scrutiny, and which disclose us as distinct persons or the sort of persons we really are. Actions uncover our values and our attitudes towards others. This is where modelling trumps knowledge, for knowledge cannot be modelled; we can only model ways of thinking, ways of learning, ways of going about things. Through our actions we model the gaze of the empire and bestow this gaze on others (i.e. strict academic standards, competition, hierarchies, etc.). As teachers, we are the most-knowledgeable-other par excellence, and our actions matter. For instance, grouping children by ability within an expected discourse of equality, could be seen as an *action* in schools that 'strive for achievement' but never publicly mention 'ability grouping' as one of their main strategies; such *action* uncovers their values. Schools, whatever their social status, need to show they *behave* within accepted social norms of inclusivity and respect. The *action* of ability grouping therefore subverts this behaviour, silently, because it uncovers the values underneath that claim: 'we nonetheless group by ability to maximise outcomes'. The Staff room is also a public space 'where people really speak and act together' (Dunne, 1997: 401), outside expected behaviour. My point here is to suggest that the ZPD and the most-knowledgeable-other work in the realm of *actions* (which includes spontaneous speech) just as much as in the context of *behaviours* or of *making*, allowing teachers to learn from each other too, thus reifying ways of being, ways of planning and delivering, ways of devaluing others, etc. Action per se has no moral compass.

Arendt (1958) refers to the 'web of human interactions' as the space where the intangibility of *actions* take place. Robert Brandom (1994) speaks of the 'space of reasons' as the foundations of language; the commitments and entitlements of speech that allow each word to sit within a web of meanings, making language of an inferential rather than representational nature. In this way, the unspoken question a child may pose, '*why* am I here?' (in this humiliating position) is answered indirectly by adults' imperial gaze and meritocratic practices, and often directly by peers, as 'is what you deserve'. Regardless of the way adults may sweeten up the experience (e.g. 'it's better for your learning', 'it will help you catch up with others', 'it's not about ability, but attainment', etc.), feeling the humiliation of the 'low ability' relegation, by any other name hurts just as much. This is because the act of grouping by ability, however we may dress it up, is already tangled in a web of human interactions and notions, like power, segregation, discrimination, humiliation. We cannot decide to give the *act* of ability grouping a new, more favourable meaning, simply by changing its name. The web of human interactions and meanings (the space of reasons) is a socio-historical event not open to change by particular, of-the-moment group discussion or by single individuals.

Arendt makes the case that, unlike a made-up story, our actual life story has no author as such, because it is revealed as we live in the web of human interactions. We may be the protagonists and heroes (the 'doers') of our life story, but the plot is not necessarily of our making. In it, we only have the power of response in the form of speech and action. For instance, if we take children in bottom sets as 'the heroes' of their own stories, we can already see that they are not there of their own choice. Meritocracy and the finer channels of power have put them there. So how do children respond? What sort of *action* serves them as enablers of resilience? Arendt observes,

> The connotation of courage, which we now feel to be an indispensable quality of the hero, is in fact already present in a willingness to act and speak at all, to insert one's self into the world and begin a story of one's own. And this courage is not necessarily or even primarily related to a willingness to suffer the consequences; courage and even boldness are already present in leaving one's hiding place and showing who one is, in disclosing and exposing one's self.
> (Arendt, 1958: 186)

As soon as children enter that place (the 'low ability' group) the school story of learning and academic achievement, wherein they once may have felt as heroes, ceases to include them. Legette observes, 'Academic identification is the extent to which schooling forms the basis of one's overall self-perception' (Legette, 2020: 1312). Children are told in so many words (through actions), that they cannot compete in the academic sphere, and worse, that they slow down the progress of the real heroes of the school story. If they misbehave in this new context, as many of them do, is not a show of courage related to any braving of consequences; it is the courage to act and speak at all in ways that subvert expected behaviour in a context that can never lead to academic achievement. The whole point of school, barring friendship, seems dissolved. If they are deemed 'not able to shine' in the school story of learning, then they need a *different* story, a story where they can indeed be the heroes and disclose themselves as subjects. How do children do this? They do it by learning it in the same way they learn anything, by observing, copying, practicing, thinking, trying on the behaviour of those who seem to succeed at the subversion. Vygotsky says,

> When children develop a method of behavior for guiding themselves that had previously been used in relation to another person, when they organize their own activities according to a social form of behavior, they succeed in applying a social attitude to themselves.
> (Vygotsky, 1978: 27)

Thus, children learn how to subvert behaviour by having access to the most-knowledgeable-other; the heroes of their own, anti-academic stories. The ZPD in bottom sets, increases the opportunities and effectiveness of such learning. The 'low ability' group thus is where alternative narratives of success are entertained, while the 'low ability' classroom is where they are fully formed and nourished.

Survival strategies in bottom sets

Teachers who can get 'bottom set' children to learn beyond set expectations, are invaluable. There is, however, a price to pay as the emotional demand and exertion of teaching bottom sets can take its toll. 'Sometimes, the best-behaved classes are your higher ability ones' (Francis et al., 2019: 125).

I recall my first bottom set. There were only 12 children in it. Most of them were white and male (there were in fact only two, very quiet girls). We might think that such a small number is easy to manage, and yet, for me, as a beginning teacher, it felt like entering a jungle where anything might happen. I say *jungle* because it was hard to see one's way clear; danger seemed to lurk in every corner as a consequence of one's inexperienced behaviours as a beginning teacher. All I had were my actions; how I responded to what I construed at the time as their challenge to authority. After that first lesson, which had been observed by their class teacher, I felt somewhat confident that I had managed to get them to do the work (French) which culminated in a group song. I knew they had been a bit noisy … but they were children after all and, they had completed the work. The teacher stood up and walked to the front of the classroom. All the children went very quiet. He said, 'I cannot believe how disrespectful you were to Miss. I would not have let you sing the song because your behaviour did not merit such a treat. I am utterly disappointed in you'. Of course, I was the one who felt embarrassed by his words. I was shocked at the discrepancy between his evaluation of the lesson and mine. How could I have been so wide of the mark? He did not have an authoritarian style and he was well-liked by the children. He was a very good teacher, so the discrepancy in our apprehensions mattered to me. In time, I realized that there was a sound reason for not letting children play with their pens, swing on their chairs, fidget too much or whisper to each other, etc. When low-level disruption is not nipped in the bud it can quickly escalate (Cogswell et al., 2020; Witham, 2020). The title of the highly popular book, *Getting the buggers to behave* (Cowley, 2010), reflects the frustration and the visceral intolerance that many adults feel when dealing with children's (mis)behaviour; children's *actions*. Sir was right: generally, nothing terrible will come from stopping children playing with their pencils and a good thing may come out of it; they might actually pay attention. Now, behaviour management strategies are only half the story. The lesson plan and our delivery of it are crucial in obvious ways; for the less engaging or accessible the lesson is, the higher the chances of having to rely on behaviour management strategies. This can make some teachers believe that ability grouping is the answer: to tailor the lesson plan to suit children's ability necessitates grouping by ability to facilitate teaching. The 'poor' behaviour in 'low ability' classes however, challenges this reasoning. 'Behaviour for learning' which claims among other things, to emphasize the 'positive social relationships that support the pupil's learning, self-worth and need for friendship' (Todd and Ellis, 2018: 130), arguing that children should be protected from failure, rejection and humiliation, fails to mention ability grouping practices as one of the main vehicles for these.

We cannot say that if we group by ability in 'sensitive' ways children won't be aware that they're being grouped by ability, nor can we claim that the practice will help their progress. The research shows that this is simply not the case (Hansen, 2008; Reay, 2017; Francis et al., 2019; Northrop and Kelly, 2019; Spina, 2019). Children know. As adults, we also know that to group by intellectual ability, particularly within close doors or within an institution is not ethical. Oxbridge lecturers may feel superior to other university lecturers, but even they would not tolerate being segregated into 'corridors of lower ability' within their own building. To group people according to their deemed 'inferior' intellectual ability constitutes an affront to human dignity, to which one is not immune by age, barring babies.

Thus, (mis)behaviour in bottom sets is notoriously common. Children will begin to knit stories of their own that give them agency over their dignities, and where academic success is but an old story. Kudos is obtained otherwise, often through the antagonization of academic learning, the prioritization of friendship over learning and the challenging of adults' role. For instance, I was never asked by my top-set students why we should be learning Spanish, but I was frequently asked this question by my middle and bottom set students. 'What's the point, Miss?' was a question I needed to prepare for. I would often say, 'How can you possibly tie your shoelaces if you don't speak Spanish?' Nonsense answers were met with less contempt than established responses like 'You never know when you might need it', 'It's good for the brain to learn a new language', 'We need to have an open mind', etc. for although the established answers are true, the school had already performed actions that excluded many children from them. The nonsense answer at least, would often get their attention if not a follow-up question. Subverting meaning seemed to strike a chord with these students. Jean Jacques Lecercle, the author of *Philosophy through the looking glass*, reminds us that

> the primary function of language is not to communicate information but to exert a force that interpellates subjects in the respective positions in which they find themselves.
>
> (2015: 4)

Information is not what these children needed from me. Like Alice in Wonderland, once children enter the bottom sets their world acquires a different North (and it is worth remembering that the Wonderland for Alice was actually a nightmare).

To counteract the humiliation of being placed in 'low ability' groups, children often misbehave or become despondent. Becoming 'uncontrollable' by teachers gives children the upper hand in something. Not all children misbehave in bottom sets, but those who do, embody the voice of revolt, which is the only action left to them, and the one that discloses them as individuals worthy of attention. Even if it is the 'wrong kind' of attention, it is the only kind worth anything by that point. As a pupil in Zevenbergen's study pointed out,

> Well, we have a teacher who can't control us and he doesn't teach us anything, so why would you want to be there. I think he might know what he has to teach us, but he doesn't teach us anything. We muck around and try to get him off the lesson. At least it makes the lesson a bit more fun.
>
> (Beechwood, Year 9) (in Zevenbergen, 2005: 616)

Epistemic revolt: turning our back on knowledge

I make a distinction here between epistemic vices and what I call epistemic revolt.

To revolt implies an enacted opposition in the name of something; 'the assertion of a limit that must not be transgressed' (Foley, 2008: 57) by those who have power over us. There is something of this in epistemic revolt, but unlike revolts of a social nature, the revolt that epistemic injustice encourages is surreptitious; like a parasite or a virus, it dwells within, making us susceptible to certain epistemic vices. We need to remember that we react—or act in Arendt's sense, unawares. Intellectual vices such as closed-mindedness or indifference to truth can be unconscious manifestations of epistemic revolt, but which nonetheless have a material impact on society's well-being. Rather than an assertion of a limit that must not be transgressed, epistemic revolt is the outcome of a transgression that already took place. Epistemic revolt is not interested in having an interlocutor as such, and thus, it is no longer a conscious assertion. As the child in the quote above said, it simply makes living a bit more fun.

For example, that someone indulges the vice of conspiracy theories without foundations is an instance of epistemic revolt. What Cassam (2018) calls 'crippled epistemology', where 'people end up believing Conspiracy Theories not because they [those people] are irrational but because they have little relevant information and their views are supported by what little they know' (Cassam, 2018: 33), is again, an example of epistemic revolt. As school children, those people may have suffered the epistemic injustice of being indirectly labelled as 'intellectually inferior', and their plight comes back to bite us all. Thus, there is a reactionary but hidden element to epistemic revolt. An unspoken anger, if you like. The Bottom Set Citizen who believes in unfounded conspiracy theories may do so precisely because these are independent of the knowledge held and 'corralled' by the establishment. Defending such theories is empowering. Cassam objects to anyone trying to 'explain away' or downplay unfounded conspiracy theories, rightly so, but he falls short of seeing (as member of an intellectual elite) his own hand in it. And yet, in his words and descriptions we can recognize the defiant, bottom set child, who has learned to seek pride elsewhere,

> The idea that the modern-day Conspiracy Theorist is capable of being intimidated will certainly amuse anyone who has had the misfortune to debate with one. Conspiracy Theorists aren't the type to be intimidated, and there is little evidence of their being silenced by establishment critics.
> (Cassam, 2018: 25)

Cassam adds later on, 'It's hard to win an argument with a person whose fundamental assumptions and ways of thinking are completely different from yours' (Cassam, 2018: 34). By using the word 'win' instead of 'have', he reveals himself as a winner. But in trying to respond to conspiracy theories he only touches marginally on aspects of education; he does not implicate educational structures of intellectual segregation in the matter. Quoting the philosopher David Hume, Cassam remarks on the emotional aspect of belief, which is, 'at least partly, a matter of feeling. Reason, Hume famously argued, is the slave of the passions' (Cassam, 2018: 40). How such passions are cultivated is worth considering. As I have been arguing in this book, children learn the value of knowledge (and the passion that may go with it) through phronesis; through the way they experience knowledge as children, not through any accompanying information. If there is any sense of accountability for epistemic vices (Battaly, 2014; Tanesini, 2021), we need to critique, at least in the school context, how children *experience* knowledge, and how some intellectual vices might be a response to epistemic injustices.

When knowledge does not pay 91

Through epistemic injustice we not only encourage epistemic revolt but also deprive children from acquiring its opposite: epistemic virtue. Epistemic virtue is the power of self-critique and re-evaluation of one's knowledge-based assumptions and prejudices, which is how we ultimately check our own actions towards others (Fricker, 2007), and how we learn to value the new understandings and growth opportunities that our intellect offers. Some epistemic virtues, like, a love of learning and a search for truth, are often fostered in 'top ability' sets. However, some epistemic and moral vices sneak in at this end too, unchecked. Feelings of superiority, intolerance, arrogance, snobbery, etc., are not uncommon perceived characteristics of children (and adults) who see themselves as possessing some kind of celebrated intellectual expertise (Milyavsky, 2017).

As far as a cohesive democracy is concerned, there are no winners in the exercise of ability grouping practices that inflate some egos while deflating others.

An interesting initiative that aims to counter this via more just educational practices, is the creation of the *Intellectual Virtues Academy* in California, which uses a lottery entry system instead of meritocratic processes. One of the ways they foster epistemic virtues, is by not tracking or grouping children by ability, which would be contrary to their ethos that stresses the role of school and classroom culture in children's thinking as a metacognitive skill. This implies, 'taking a new stance toward teaching, of changing the story of learning one is

Figure 5.2 Intellectual Virtues Academy (website), California.
Source: IVA (2023).

telling, and reconceptualizing the goals of education' (Ritchhart and Church, 2020: 10). In this way the message that is enacted does not deny protagonism to anyone (Figure 5.2). However, US states that are less progressive and have strong conservative values, are more likely to sustain the imperial gaze around knowledge and power due to the unfair hierarchies that meritocracy encourages through ability grouping practices, turning many children into education's anti-heroes.

Concluding thoughts

Not all children in bottom sets are visibly antagonistic towards adults. Particularly girls. Some may internalize an anti-academic story that quietly complies with adults' world. When wealth (extra tutoring, support, and resources) is not enough to get some children out of a bottom set, their plight cannot be blamed on anything other than their supposed, actual lack of intellectual ability. Wealthy children may have vast connections that allow them to find self-esteem elsewhere, but this does not mean they have not been harbouring a secret epistemic revolt of their own, an anti-academic narrative to hold onto. Children from disadvantaged backgrounds might at least have the recourse of a social injustice as answerable for their plight. Even so, unless they have other talents, their lot is often a much more challenging one. A certain relation has been found between gang membership and disengagement from education (Beckett et al., 2013; Children's Commissioner for England, 2017). We could say that many children acquire a warped academic identification, learning to see themselves as 'not as able' to learn and therefore of diminished value, for if we humiliate anyone—and we shouldn't—we tend to humiliate those who we feel 'deserve it' or have implicitly no value to us. In this sense, whereas we may easily appreciate the plight of children from disadvantaged backgrounds coming up against 'middle-class morality' (the kind of morality usually desired by schools), we may miss and dismiss the humiliation that wealthier children may suffer, but as we'll see in Chapter 7, we ignore this to our peril.

I have argued so far, that placing children in 'low ability' sets is the way in which alternative narratives of success find room to flourish; that the ZPD and the most-knowledgeable-other become instruments of a different kind of learning, which favours an anti-academic story. This allows children to gain a purpose-built sense of agency and self-esteem, where they begin to experience the importance of social kudos and the irrelevance of academic effort. I remember a boy who, in my presence, attempted to break into my classroom cupboard with the intention of retrieving his friend's Hip-Hop cap (which I had confiscated following school regulations). His act was a courageous act of friendship first and foremost. That it was disrespectful and somewhat aggressive is the privileged adults' take on it. I was not a friend, and in his eyes probably a foe. He was a hero and resilient in ways adults cannot appreciate; a hero who had rightly turned his back on any sense of academic pursuit, for who wants to pursue failure and humiliation? To think along the lines of Arthur Doolittle, the boy could not afford (or did not see the point) to engage in the niceties of the intellectual elites' morality. In children's impressionable eyes, when school acts in questionable ways towards them, it forfeits their respect.

References

Abtahi, Y., Graven, M., & Lerman, S. (2017). Conceptualising the more knowledgeable other within a multi-directional ZPD. *Educational Studies in Mathematics*, *96*(3), 275–287.

Arendt, H. (1958). *The human condition (Charles R. Walgreen Foundation Lectures)* (3rd Printing). University of Chicago Press.

Battaly, H. (2014). Varieties of epistemic vice. In J. Matheson & R. Vitz (Eds.), *The ethics of belief* (pp. 51–76). Oxford University Press.

Beckett, H., Brodie, I., Factor, F., Melrose, M., Pearce, J. J., Pitts, J., Shuker, L., & Warrington, C. (2013). *'It's wrong—But you get used to it': A qualitative study of gang-associated sexual violence towards, and exploitation of, young people in England* [Technical Report]. University of Bedfordshire.

Brandom, R. (1994). *Making it explicit: Reasoning, representing & discursive commitment: Reasoning, representing and discursive commitment*. Harvard University Press.

Cassam, Q. (2018, February 28). Epistemic vices and conspiracy theories. Blog of the APA.

Children's Commissioner for England. (2017). *Children's voices: A review of evidence on the subjective wellbeing of children involved in gangs in England*. Children's Commissioner for England.

The Children's Society. (2023). *What is emotional resilience?* The Children's Society. www.childrenssociety.org.uk/information/young-people/well-being/resources/emotional-resilience

Cogswell, S., Carr, A., Abbott, N., & Monks, C. P. (2020). The development and validation of a teacher-reported low-level classroom disruption scale (LLCD-S). *Emotional and Behavioural Difficulties*, *25*(3–4), 230–243.

Cowley, S. (2010). *Getting the buggers to behave*. Bloomsbury Publishing.

Davis, R. (2011, July 25). School colour-codes pupils by ability. *The Guardian.* www.theguardian.com/education/2011/jul/25/secondary-school-streaming

Department for Education and Skills. (2005). *The behaviour and attendance action plan toolkit. Unit 3. Dealing with consistently poor behaviour.* Department for Education and Skills.

Derry, J. (2006). What is it to be a human knower? *Philosophy Now, 63,* 10–11.

Didau, D. (2016, November 14). *Bottom sets and the scourge of low-level disruption.* David Didau.

Dunne, J. (1997). Hannah Arendt's distinction between action and making in the human condition. In *Back to the Rough Ground* (pp. 88–103). University of Notre Dame Press.

Eun, B. (2019). The zone of proximal development as an overarching concept: A framework for synthesizing Vygotsky's theories. *Educational Philosophy and Theory, 51*(1), 18–30.

Foley, J. (2008). *Albert Camus: From the absurd to revolt.* Taylor & Francis Group.

Francis, B., Taylor, B., Tereshchenko, A., Taylor, B., & Tereshchenko, A. (2019). *Reassessing 'Ability' grouping: Improving practice for equity and attainment.* Routledge.

Fricker, M. (2007). Epistemic injustice: Power and the ethics of knowing. In *Epistemic injustice.* Oxford University Press.

Hansen, B. (2008). Is the bluebird really a phoenix? Ability grouping seems to rise from the ashes ad infinitum. *Reading Today, 25*(6), 19–20.

IVA. (2023). *Intellectual Virtues Academy.* www.ivalongbeach.org/

Lecercle, J.-J. (2015). Language is worth a thousand pounds a word. *Angles. New Perspectives on the Anglophone World, 1,* Article 1.

Legette, K. (2020). A social-cognitive perspective of the consequences of curricular tracking on youth outcomes. *Educational Psychology Review, 32*(3), 885–900.

Luković, S., Marinković, B., & Zotović-Kostić, M. (2022). The zone of actual and the zone of proximal development measured through preschool dynamic assessment as predictors of later school performance—A longitudinal study. *Psihologija, 55*(1), 89–105.

Milyavsky, M., Kruglanski, A. W., Chernikova, M., & Schori-Eyal, N. (2017). Evidence for arrogance: On the relative importance of expertise, outcome, and manner. *PLOS One, 12*(7), e0180420–e0180420.

Northrop, L., & Kelly, S. (2019). Who gets to read what? Tracking, instructional practices, and text complexity for middle school struggling readers. *Reading Research Quarterly, 54*(3), 339–361.

Reay, D. (2017). *Miseducation: Inequality, education and the working classes* (1st ed.). Policy Press.

Ritchhart, R., & Church, M. (2020). *The power of making thinking visible: Practices to engage and empower all learners* (1st ed.). Jossey-Bass, a Wiley Brand.

Spina, N. (2019). 'Once upon a time': Examining ability grouping and differentiation practices in cultures of evidence-based decision-making. *Cambridge Journal of Education, 49*(3), 329–348. https://doi.org/10.1080/0305764X.2018.1533525

Suissa, J. (2015). Character education and the disappearance of the political. *Ethics and Education, 10*(1), 105–117.

Tanesini, A. (2021). Wrongs, responsibility, blame, and oppression. In A. Tanesini (Ed.), *The mismeasure of the self: A study in vice epistemology*. Oxford University Press.

Tod, J., & Ellis, S. (2018). *Behaviour for learning: Promoting positive relationships in the classroom* (2nd ed.). Routledge.

Vygotsky, L. S. (1978). *Mind in society: The development of higher psychological processes; edited by Michael Cole [and 3 others]*. Harvard University Press.

Weare, K. (2015). *What works in promoting social and emotional well-being and responding to mental health problems in schools?* National Children's Bureau.

Witham, S. A. (2020). *Addressing the elephant in the room: Managing low-level disruption in the primary classroom*. ProQuest Dissertations Publishing.

Zevenbergen, R. (2005). The construction of a mathematical habitus: Implications of ability grouping in the middle years. *Journal of Curriculum Studies, 37*(5), 607–619.

6 The rise of the bottom set citizen

A dispersed non-community: meritocracy's undeserving

'What's the point?'

I still remember my mentor's words when he decided to exclude the Spanish bottom set class from a university visitor's talk. Michael Young's dystopian prediction for a meritocratic society was that it would ultimately lead to resentment on the part of the 'lower intellectual classes' and dangerously succumb to chaos and violence. Epistemic revolt, however, is not an up-in-arms sort of reaction, but rather, an insidious resistance that can equally lead to chaos when perversely manipulated. As Allen remarked, 'A society that is *justly unequal* invites rebellion in a way that an *unjustly unequal* society does not' (Allen, 2011: 375). Thus, the intellectual meritocracy's *undeserving*, although different in kind to the old-world order of so called 'undeserving poor', suffer a similar contempt.

The Cambridge dictionary defines the *undeserving poor* as 'people who are poor because of their own actions and should not get sympathy from other people'. Mr Alfred Doolittle, a character conceived by Shaw (1913 and fleshed out as Eliza's father in the film My Fair Lady (1964), is a clever example of the old world-order of the *undeserving poor*: an intelligent, working-class individual with no education, who, as he says, is not only one of the 'undeserving poor' but also constantly 'up against middle-class morality' (by which in the United Kingdom context really means the privileged, 'upper class'[1] morality). Doolittle however, has the advantage of having suffered a social rather than an epistemic injustice. As the victim of a social injustice, Doolittle can lament only the lack of opportunity or ambition to become as good as anyone else. Had he been a child of our times he may not have had that recourse, for in our view of meritocracy, opportunities are supposed to abound, even if only in myth form. Lack of success these days is assumed to be only attributed to the individual who squandered the opportunities offered. We know now that intelligence is only one of many aspects that may contribute to the opportunity for social mobility, which has itself been criticized as a 'form of cruel optimism' (Raey, 2017: 102), but in Young's meritocracy, the 'low classes' (workers and technicians) knew, by repeated I.Q. testing, that in a perverse way they deserved to be where they were. Young (in character) retorts,

> We do not need to ask why. The schools have begun to do their proper job of social selection—that is all. Once the long-called-for reforms were made, none of the ablest children in the country, unless by an unfortunate mistake, had to take up manual work.
>
> (Young, 1994: 134)

'Unfortunate mistakes', a generous term, happen only too often these days. Many intelligent children who for some reason do not fit the 'academic' mould end up in 'low ability' groups. Had young Alfred Doolittle lived in Young's meritocracy, he may have been creamed off the poor classes and educated as part of an intellectual elite. Others would not have been so fortunate and would thus become automatic members of the 'low intellectual classes'; people who can no longer pretend their lot is down to lack of opportunity, for school has told them, time and time again, that,

> their image of themselves is more nearly a true, unflattering, reflection. Are they not bound to recognize that they have an inferior status—not as in the past because they were denied opportunity; but because they *are* inferior? For the first time in human history the inferior man has no ready buttress for his self-regard. ... Men who have lost their self-respect are liable to lose their inner vitality. ... and may only too easily cease to be either good citizens or good technicians.
>
> (Young, 1994: 97)

But that was Young's meritocracy. The meritocracy of our times does not have the same extreme and blatant principles of Michael Young's apocalyptic view (Allen, 2011). We do not go about testing youngsters' intelligence and treating them accordingly and regardless of social class—or do we? It was in fact the high I.Q. parents of 'lower' I.Q. children in Young's meritocracy, who were the first to complain. They saw themselves (their children's fate) adversely affected by a 'just' meritocracy. The real trouble began there; with the discontent of the powerful who began to infiltrate the ranks of the working classes, who in turn, were 'only too easily' led to revolt. When the revolts began, the narrator reflects that,

> The hostility now manifest has long been latent. For more than half a century, the lower classes have been harbouring resentments which they could not make articulate, until the present day.
>
> (Young, 1994: 78)

With the intellectual help, that is, of the elites.

The type of revolt that epistemic injustices fosters is radically different from those derived from social ones. Faced with a social injustice, we can fervently identify with others in terms of our deplorable or unjust circumstances, and collectively fight without losing or sacrificing our self-esteem. Epistemic injustices on the other hand, are of an insidious nature, covertly caused and hence hidden like a secret revolt that cannot articulate its own name.

Whether in Young's dystopian fantasy or in our own lives, no one wishes to be associated, identified or united under the banner of so called 'low intellectual classes'. Whatever one's age, being placed in a 'low ability' group cuts deep. As a six-year-old in a London primary school expressed,

> *They [the Lions] think they are better than us. They think they are good at every single thing and the second group, Tigers, there are some people who think they good and more important than us. And one of the boys in Giraffes he was horrible to me and he said "get lost slow tortoise" but my group are Monkeys and we are only second to bottom.*
>
> (Raey, 2017: 79)

Having one's self-esteem knocked about by adults; by 'those who know', those who in so many words yield knowledge as a weapon, makes knowledge itself a target of contempt. Thus, the revolt that epistemic injustice encourages, unlike social injustices (i.e. lack of

The rise of the bottom set citizen 99

access to education or health) is not of an 'up in arms' sort, but rather a silent treatment, a looking away, a cold shoulder. Epistemic revolt is the expression of an explicit indifference and disdain towards institutionalized forms of knowledge (i.e. this book) and towards those who thrive through them in the establishment: anyone with a university education; top set citizens and *Lions* of the adult world, too quick to look down on the perceived 'uneducated'. Academic standards, the fortress of meritocracy's intellectual elites, is a kind of fail-safe system that keeps the presumed 'intellectually undeserving' at arms' length. It is not difficult to see how either resentment or numbness begins to find a home in young people's dispositions towards 'knowledge'.

Further thoughts on John Dewey's ideas on democracy in education

A reconceptualization of the work by American psychologist, philosopher, and educator John Dewey, particularly his writings on Democracy in Education (1916), allows us to broaden our understanding of the role of school in education (Heilbronn et al., 2018). If Dewey is correct and school is where children acquire, as evolving citizens, the democratic practices of society (Carpenter, 2006), and if schools are, 'environments framed with express reference to influencing the mental and moral disposition of their members' (Dewey, 1916: 22), then school is the place where many children are shaped as future bottom set citizens (BSCs), ripe for epistemic revolt.

The concept of what it means to be a citizen in a democracy is, in Dewey's terms, educationally relevant. For in a democracy,

> The heart of the matter is found not in the voting nor in counting the votes to see where the majority is formed. It is in the *process* by which they're formed.
>
> (Dewey, in Bernstein, 2010: 290, my italics)

This process starts in the home and the community, but it is in the school's day-to-day transactions (Willis, 1978) that children learn what it means to be alone (without parents) in the world and how to begin to represent oneself to the world, as an emergent citizen in a democracy. Except that, as discussed in Chapter 3, schools are autocratic systems. Citizenship is thus, experienced rather than learned within an autocratic system. John Dewey is a familiar voice in teacher education. He emphasizes the potential of the social studies to this end, stressing the idea of designing a curriculum that operates from and with the child's experiences as opposed to being merely information-based, as is still usually the case.

> Students learning only isolated facts would be "the easy prey of skilful politicians and political machines; the victims of political misrepresentation" (Dewey, 1973, p.185) … unable to differentiate fact from opinion even as reported in the daily newspapers. The information-based form of civic education would not lead to "intelligent voting" or to "intelligent legislation".
>
> (Carpenter, 2006: 36)

I claimed in previous chapters however, that it is schools' organization around teaching and learning that informs children's experiences much more than the curriculum does. Dewey stressed the social school life of the child as integral to their education, but he worked on the assumption that teachers and schools would approach civic education at the curriculum or activity level. Teachers in the United Kingdom, for instance, are encouraged to design lessons that allow children to make connections between a subject and their daily experiences (this is fortuitously aided by the absence of rigid textbooks in the United Kingdom). The problem, however, seems to be at the school structural level. Teaching citizenship, either discreetly or through the social sciences, can still be ineffective if other more powerful school *actions*, like ability grouping, are at work. When Dewey speaks of 'isolated facts' he doesn't mean facts isolated from the subject context, but from the child's context of experience, and this isolation also speaks to the taken-for-granted practices within the school (Heilbronn et al., 2018). Subjects or initiatives around 'character formation', 'growth mindset', or 'citizenship' are not learned by children discreetly, but through experience; through all the things that happen and are said through, under and between lessons, or in Arendt's terms, through *actions*. In other words, citizenship is contextually learned through the way the teaching organization is taken up, which reflects the values of a society (Biesta, 2010), including child participation and teachers' own habits and dispositions (Alderson, 2004; Nelsen, 2015). Regardless of the lesson content, activities, discussions, ample playing fields, or of how broad or well delivered a curriculum may be, children learn what it means to be a member of a society by the way they are *treated* and the way they see others being treated in school. For instance, evaluating Australia's Ethical Understanding Curriculum for ages 4–17, Bleazby (2020) observes that children are asked to enquire, evaluate, formulate, and adopt desirable moral values and attributes (Bleazby, 2020). However, how does this fit with children's (moot point) experiences of being grouped by ability in the same school that professes to instil moral values? I imagine that the school does succeed at least in instilling values around feelings of inferiority or superiority in children. Children in Year 2 are to be encouraged for example to 'discuss ethical concepts within a range of familiar contexts' (Bleazby, 2020: 88), but I wager that 'should we be grouped by ability in school' is not one of them, however familiar the experience may be. We know what children would say (like the little girl's eloquent response earlier) because we know what *we* would say under similar circumstances.

Such contradiction tends to warp rather than help build what John Dewey saw as positive mental and moral dispositions. Children will look for full acceptance and 'full membership' elsewhere. Research has already pointed, for example, towards a connection between disengagement with education, training or employment and gang culture (Beckett et al., 2013). Other studies have carried out extensive interviews with young gang members,

> Children did not always join gangs out of choice; some viewed it as an inevitability based on where they lived, others reported a lack of opportunity and status in society as push factors. This lack of opportunity and feeling of powerlessness was commonly reported by young people.
> (Children's Commissioner for England, 2017: 28)

Working-class boys appear to be particularly affected by loss of status and reported the 'sense of powerlessness and educational worthlessness, and feeling that they were not really valued and respected within education' (Raey, 2017: 80).

Connecting the humiliation experienced through epistemic injustice to children's behaviour as young adults, allow us to appreciate the way society shapes many children as 'lesser' intellectual citizens who grow up to become BSCs once they come of age. As I have argued previously, survival and achievement in bottom sets, unsurprisingly, have little to do with academic effort, which is ruled out by default. Self-esteem is thus harnessed through opposition, resistance, and defiance towards an establishment repleted with an intellectually meritocratic elite.

Children placed in 'low ability' groups are not encouraged towards epistemic virtue; towards the idea that formalized knowledge can enrich our lives whatever we pursue; towards the possibility to reason fact from fiction; to have informed opinions and ideas that lead to effective democratic processes. Attempting an appreciation of learning has merited them little success and often bestowed its opposite: dismissal and derision. Such children may find solace outside educational contexts, engaging with what bestows them a sense of worth as valued members of any given community.

Children from advantaged backgrounds who are nonetheless constantly placed in bottom sets can also feel a sense of isolation ... but their plight is seldom a focus of research, perhaps they seem to be otherwise (at least financially) 'cushioned' from the blow, or perhaps consent from their parents is not easily obtained. However, when all the wealth in the world cannot get you out of a 'low ability' group, one's narrative of self-esteem is challenged completely. The lower economic classes may have the advantage here sometimes, particularly when children are born in circles where there is a salient, extended family, and community support, morally, emotionally, and socially (i.e. Williams, 2023; see also literature that engages with Critical Race Theory, i.e. Dixson et al., 2014; and literature on the necessity of youth clubs, i.e. Middleton, 2021). For vulnerable children without community support however, gang culture can thrive as the only 'welcoming' alternative. It is by no means easy being a gang member or associated with one (particularly for girls, see Bryant, 2023). Children as young as 12, begin to develop defences that precipitate them towards 'opting out' of hopes and engagement with education (Francis et al., 2019).

Among the initiatives that have been put in place to address gang involvement, schools' teaching and learning structures of intellectual hierarchies are never challenged.

Social media and the idea of empowerment

There seems to be a public perception that social media is empowering. A general belief that social media can bestow a sense of agency and control to those who may not have been able to feel empowered before. Anyone—provided they have access to social media, can have a public platform these days, and the audience is the world. However, social media is a two-faced platform. It is a place where the supposed 'freedom of expression' gives equal space to truths and deceptions that lead to freedom of oppression. The idea of empowerment, having positive connotations (emancipation, dignity, agency, etc.) wraps all deception as potential truths that benefit us, and any unwelcome truth as potential deceptions that harm us. Social media empowers us to decide on truths effortlessly, based solely on our opinions (Vaast et al., 2014; Selwyn, 2016; Tye et al., 2019; Seneviratne, 2020; Hurley, 2021).

In academic circles we can critique the dubious idea of 'social media as empowering' ad nauseam, but it will have very little effect on the general public's perception of social media as a personal and collective good. After all, it has helped harness collective discontent so as to challenge oppressive governments around the world (Arab Spring in 2011; Occupy Wall Street in 2011; Hong Kong's The Umbrella Movement in 2014; Chilean social revolt in 2019). Tye et al. (2019) explore the Bersih movement in Malaysia in 2014, as being one such example, enabled by social media at the grass roots level; a bottom-up collective action. They elaborate on the essential distinctions made between *collective* versus *connective* action,

> The logic of connective action argues for a more expansive path to concerted actions through the self-motivated sharing of personalised content on social media—it allows dispersed individuals to come together spontaneously even if they do not all identify with a common ideology or collective identity and even if membership and organisational resources are not present a priori.
> (Tye et al., 2019: 173)

This *connective* as opposed to collective action, has no social norms, no reason to be other than for the connection itself, and therefore it has no social agenda as such. All it requires is a starting and an end point. It provides exactly what the 'non-community' of dispersed BSCs need: a platform that does not identify them as anything in particular, let alone a collective 'academically intellectual inferior'; the grassroots of educational marginalization. There is no self-identified elite groups (Benford, 1997) within the ranks of BS citizenry that one could find and interview to gain insight into their movement.

104 *The rise of the bottom set citizen*

Referring to the most 'tweeted' topic of 2010, the oil spill in the Gulf of Mexico, Vaast et al. warn us about the unpredictable framing of discourse and the growing mistrust towards 'established actors' (organized institutions) in the public arena,

> when **framing** comes from multiple, anonymous, and dispersed **actors**, it may instead lead to further question and doubt **established actors** and the handling of the **crisis**.
>
> (Vaast et al., 2014: 909, their bold)

It is all very well to praise the so-called, empowering nature of social media, as long as it does not directly affect organized forms of knowledge (the establishment, the West, giant corporations, etc.). However, social media's sharp end, unlike a knife, seldom has an identifiable actor wielding it. Things can be said, denied, re-sent, liked, hated, all anonymously; connecting us to others at a visceral level; creating flash mobs or lynch mobs alike. When people have access, social media empowers everyone and nobody at the same time. As Hurley (2021) found out, voicing one's thoughts is not necessarily a sign of empowerment,

> This is because power and its displays via self-presentations are entangled within hyper-inequalities, political discrimination, environmental destruction, homophobia, racism, and gender oppression embedded within the post digital condition.
>
> (Hurley, 2021: 12)

together with the entanglement of epistemic injustices; the social construction of many children as lesser-learner-come-citizens, displaying and expressing themselves in the only media that embraces them fully.

Bottom set citizen of the post-truth nation

'There is much incentive and little penalty for improving the "narrative" of one's life'. Says Ralph Keyes in his website, author of *The post-truth era: dishonesty and deception in contemporary life* (2004). The term he coined as 'post-truth era', an age where feeling and personal beliefs weigh more than facts, has more than delivered on his original warning, or so it seemed during the storming of the US Capitol Hill in 2021. Twenty years later, his words and the whole idea

The rise of the bottom set citizen 105

of post-truth has even greater resonance. Horsthemke (2017) insightfully holds the intellectual elites responsible at least for relativizing the concept of (Western) truth and bringing it to the level of cultural practices, perspective, subjectivity, which the public imagination then sees as individual practices too, why not? With so many sources of diverse information available there is more room to disagree.

The words by a columnist of The Times of India (a country whose marked hierarchical class system was supported and consolidated during the British Empire rule), served Seneviratne (2020) to make a point regarding the idea that evidence for any opinions in the post-truth era is easily found,

> 'There is no floor to stand on, no basis for certainty' notes Gopalakrishnan, adding 'while the nature of disagreements isn't new, the Internet has intensified the breakdown of objective assessment'. So what this has led to is that when we have a gut sense, a received belief system, we then find evidence to support it.
>
> (Seneviratne, 2020: 108)

For children who were shaped into adult BSCs, improving one's narrative through denial and subversion of facts, not only provides a much-needed respite but is a highly accessible and enjoyable option too. This quiet revolt that epistemic injustice engenders, is one that at best ignores organized forms of knowledge and at worst subverts them by producing alternative facts; by demoting academic knowledge to mere opinion. Schools and universities, as the organized institutions of academic knowledge par excellence, become not a target of attention, but its opposite, a specific target of (mis)attention in the individual's adult life. For how do we cope with a source of pain that can never be brought to justice, because it claims to know all about justice?

Mark Mlawer, an educational resources director, was struck in 1994 by the content of a slogan that hits out to the academic elite. In the United States, students assessed as 'academically able' are placed in *honour* classes, while the rest are left with clear messages about their intellectual (in)abilities (Legette, 2018). Mlawer says,

> First, the honor roll, it seems to me, is a tradition which reinforces some of the least attractive aspects of our culture, and for that reason should be eliminated or radically altered. ... As to the parents who brag through their car bumpers and the schools that promote such

106 *The rise of the bottom set citizen*

behavior, other parents are starting to respond. "My Kid Beat Up Your Honor Student": This slogan, which I encountered recently, helps clarify this issue. Self-esteem and pride can come from many sources; and resentment at the unfairness of the honor roll and at those who flaunt their child's academic feats causes some parents to take pride where they can find it.

(1994)

Feeling empowered by physical prowess or through social media is one possible source of pride for the 'intellectually disenfranchised'; meritocracy's undeserving. The only way to revolt against institutionalized forms of knowledge is to actively ignore them where we can; to mistrust their information or tamper with it; to trust any information if it's relatable (not abstract in any way); to distribute information as competing truths, etc. In other words, to use Howard Frankfurt's (2005) term, to raise 'bullshit' to new heights of acceptance; to obscure its very name in order to pass it as 'truth'. But then, we, as representatives of academic knowledge, are in no position to blame anybody, after all, BSCs learned disparagement from us. We were already talking humbug ourselves when, as educators and bearers of knowledge, we humiliated them through ability grouping practices while proclaiming to instil in them 'good' morals and values. Referring to the promised land of the advancement in education through technology, Selwyn (2016) emphasizes the disconnect between rhetoric and practice,

> Perhaps, the fundamental problem with the bullshit of education and technology is what Frankfurt identifies as the inherent disconnect from 'how things really are'.
>
> (439)

When Horsthemke makes the following statement, he is careful to leave open the possibility that some educators might indeed show such disconnect, and in fact not be truthful and sincere in their interactions with children,

> While something might be said for teaching strategies that are not directly truth-promoting, like playing devil's advocate or trying on an argument for size, good practice is arguably modelled by

educators who pursue truth and who are truthful and sincere in their interactions with others.

(Horsthemke, 2017: 280)

And likewise, the opposite is hence also true: bad practice can be modelled too.

'How things really are' in the educational experience of our children, is often invisible to the adults who have succeeded at the knowledge game: the intellectual elites. Childhood studies are inevitably always carried out by outsiders: adults who don't know what it's like to be labelled as 'intellectually inferior' or whatever the euphemism of their time. Unfortunately, the belief in meritocratic practices obscures the tragedy as well as any potential ways out, and 'those who know' know it well, such understanding, 'is widely shared across the political spectrum' (Civil and Himsworth, 2020: 377), as well as by some in the teaching profession. One of the teachers in Raey's study observed how the only thing worse than having to teach in the system as it is, was being a child at its mercy. I have already discussed in previous chapters why those who know the situation are unable or unwilling to change it (meritocracy's allegiance to imperial values around competition and hierarchies); what 'feels right' or seems 'common-sense' needs no research evidence either way. Those whose interests and power are sustained by meritocratic practices need no reason to raise the question, unless, like the 'high classes' in Young's meritocracy, they see their own children adversely affected when delegated to the bottom sets or equivalent. The only difference I see in this respect, is that a wealthy BSC is far more dangerous than a poor one. Just imagine having the power and means, as a single person, of demoting facts to mere opinion. God forbid.

Concluding thoughts

Our belief in meritocracy in education, when coupled with ability grouping practices can stop some children from developing epistemic virtue. Thus, as adults, meritocracy's *undeserving* find common ground, anonymously, through social media and the empowerment it claims to bestow, offering refuge for those who felt intellectually disfranchised by the establishment. BSCs belong to a connective, dispersed non-community no one wants to be an identifiable member of.

I have argued that the BSC sits awkwardly in a democratic society that proclaims equality of opportunity, due to its dubious meritocratic practices that mingle humiliation with epistemic injustices, forcing children to find self-esteem and acceptance outside educational contexts, and often in direct opposition to the instrument of humiliation: formalized knowledge. The post-truth nation is the only nation that fully embraces the BSC we helped create; a nation where the intellectual elites are stripped of power and status, and ironically delegated to the bottom set of relativism and alternative facts; where all information is potentially just someone's dismissible opinion (epistemic revolt).

The rise of the BSC is of our own making.

Note

1 Unlike in most other countries, 'middle-classes' in UK are composed of an intellectual elite, usually of middle to high income.

References

Alderson, P. (2004). Democracy in schools: Myths, mirages and making it happen. In B. Linsley & E. Rayment (Eds.), *Beyond the classroom: Exploring active citizenship in 11–16 education*. New Politics Network.

Allen, A. (2011). Michael Young's the Rise of the Meritocracy: A philosophical critique. *British Journal of Educational Studies*, 59(4), 367–382.

Beckett, H., Brodie, I., Factor, F., Melrose, M., Pearce, J. J., Pitts, J., Shuker, L., & Warrington, C. (2013). *'It's wrong—But you get used to it': A qualitative study of gang-associated sexual violence towards, and exploitation of, young people in England* [Technical Report]. University of Bedfordshire.

Benford, R. D. (1997). An insider's critique of the social movement framing perspective. *Sociological Inquiry*, 67(4), 409–430.

Bernstein, R. J. (2010). Dewey's vision of radical democracy. In M. Cochran (Ed.), *The Cambridge companion to Dewey* (pp. 288–308). Cambridge University Press.

Biesta, G. J. J. (2010). Why 'what works' still won't work: From evidence-based education to value-based education. *Studies in Philosophy and Education*, 29(5), 491–503.

Bleazby, J. (2020). Fostering moral understanding, moral inquiry & moral habits through philosophy in schools: A Deweyian analysis of Australia's Ethical Understanding curriculum. *Journal of Curriculum Studies*, 52(1), 84–100.

Bryant, M. (2023, October 4). 'They didn't believe my life': The poet from the centre of Sweden's gang wars. *The Guardian*.

Carpenter, J. J. (2006). 'The Development of a More Intelligent Citizenship': John Dewey and the social studies. *Education and Culture, 22*(2), 31–42.

Children's Commissioner for England. (2017). *Children's voices: A review of evidence on the subjective wellbeing of children involved in gangs in England*. Children's Commissioner for England.

Civil, D., & Himsworth, J. J. (2020). Introduction: Meritocracy in perspective. The rise of the meritocracy 60 years on. *Political Quarterly, 91*(2), 373–378.

Dewey, J. (1916). *Democracy and education*. The Macmillan Company.

Dixson, A. D., Rousseau Anderson, C. K., Donnor, J. K., & Anderson, C. K. R. (2014). *Critical race theory in education: All God's children got a song*. Routledge.

Francis, B., Taylor, B., Tereshchenko, A., Taylor, B., & Tereshchenko, A. (2019). *Reassessing 'Ability' grouping: Improving practice for equity and attainment*. Routledge.

Frankfurt, H. G. (2005). On Bullshit. In *On Bullshit* (pp. 1–68). Princeton University Press.

Heilbronn, R., Doddington, C., & Higham, R. (2018). *Dewey and education in the 21st century: Fighting back*. Emerald Publishing Limited.

Horsthemke, K. (2017). '#FactsMustFall'?—Education in a post-truth, post-truthful world. *Ethics and Education, 12*(3), 273–288.

Hurley, Z. (2021). Reimagining Arab women's social media empowerment and the postdigital condition. *Social Media + Society, 7*(2), 205630512110101.

Keyes, R. (2004). *The post-truth era: Dishonesty and deception in contemporary life*. St. Martin's Publishing Group.

Legette, K. (2018). School tracking and youth self-perceptions: Implications for academic and racial identity. *Child Development, 89*(4), 1311–1327.

Mlawer, M. A. (1994). My kid beat up your honor student. *Education Week*.

Middleton, L. (2021). *Overlooked: Young people and rural youth services (National Youth Agency Final Report)*. https://static.nya.org.uk/static/d15ff8e9b33bd4cff7b138043e50a358/Overlooked-Report-NYA-Final.pdf

Nelsen, P. J. (2015). Intelligent dispositions: Dewey, habits and inquiry in teacher education. *Journal of Teacher Education, 66*(1), 86–97.

Reay, D. (2017). *Miseducation: inequality, education and the working classes* (1st ed.). Policy Press.

Selwyn, N. (2016). *Is technology good for education?*. Polity.

Seneviratne, K. (2020). *Myth of 'free media' and fake news in the post-truth era* (1st ed.). SAGE Publications India.

Shaw, G. B. (1913). *Pygmalion*. https://en.wikipedia.org/w/index.php?title=Pygmalion_(play)&oldid=1167169723

Tye, M., Leong, C., Pan, S. L., Bahri, S., & Fauzi, A. (2019). Social media empowerment in social movements: Power activation and power accrual in digital activism. *European Journal of Information Systems, 28*(2), 173–204.

Vaast, E., Safadi, H., Negoita, B., & Lapointe, L. (2014). Grassroots versus established actors' framing of a crisis: Tweeting the oil spill. *Academy of Management Proceedings*, *2014*(1), 13655.

Williams, B. (2023). Demolition derby, working-class identity, and capitalist geographies. *Journal of Working-Class Studies*, *8*(1), Article 1.

Willis, P. (1978). Monday morning and the millennium. In *Learning to labour*. Routledge.

Young, M. D. (1994). *The rise of the meritocracy / Michael Young; with a new introduction by the author* (New ed.). Transaction.

7 'It never did me any harm'
Some BSC exemplars

Ethical consideration: on exhibiting injustices

I have often walked under Finsbury Park bridge in London and seen homeless people sleeping on cardboard and mattresses on the pavement, covered in blankets and discarded tents. Such a site is not uncommon around 'developed' cities in the West. It is the surrounding wealth that highlights them. I always get the feeling that we failed the homeless when they were children. I imagine what they would have looked like then; what could have been done differently on all sides, that *one* of those sides may have made a difference. I speak in this book of the school side of things, which forms no small part in a child's life. Children from disadvantaged backgrounds tend to be overrepresented in 'low ability' sets. The social and emotional injustices they may have received leave them more vulnerable to suffer epistemic ones too. The blows of childhood can resonate throughout one's life, so whenever we attempt to exhibit such blows, we must be careful.

There are some ethical considerations here that I wish to express. I claim that bottom set citizens (BSCs) exist across social class, and the first two examples I use, Nigel Farage and Donald Trump, are clear examples of privileged upbringings, a fact which may somewhat cushion the blow of being made to feel academically 'inferior' to others. The blow, nonetheless, was at one point a real one.

The first ethical consideration is that Farage and Trump, as well as the homeless, do not deserve our contempt, for contempt only manages to make matters worse and is often met by a different kind of contempt towards us, twice as high. Some may object that I place Farage or Trump in a similar category to the homeless—to the detriment of the latter. If I do so, it is only because all of them were once children, and as a society we failed all of them. Neither am I saying that the homeless are an example of BSC. I simply mention them because as children and young adults, they have often been the recipients of social and emotional injustices, and thus are often the focus of research (O'Mahony, 1988; D'Ath et al., 2016; Kyprianides et al., 2021; Craven et al., 2022). Research usually brings to the fore those who have been at the receiving end of injustices, thus inevitably reifying victimhood profiles, while identified perpetrators often remain invisible behind societal structures.

That Farage and Trump are victims at all may take some convincing. But we are familiar with the African proverb, 'It takes a village to raise a child', so if I present them here as victims it is to do with our share of the responsibility. We, as educators or members of an intellectual elite, have made some children and adults feel inferior. I shine the spotlight of victimhood and deficit on the rich for a change, not because they are victims now, in need of our sympathy or help, but because they were victims once, and because we may have unwittingly contributed to their actions now. Trump and Farage are my personified examples of BSCs, because they are powerful BSCs and thus can have enormous impact on vulnerable, powerless ones. We overlook the wealthy BSC at our peril. No child deserves the intellectual scorn of others, particularly when it comes with adult sanction, albeit indirectly.

The second ethical dilemma I face is that it seems unethical to search and identify adults who may have been labelled as 'low ability' group/class members for most of their school life. No one wishes to receive the public spotlight on their potential humiliation. On the contrary, we tend to hide or dismiss information that shames us. My dilemma is that I cannot 'use' as an example of BSC someone who is already vulnerable.

I agree with the need to avoid the reification of victimhood; of, for instance,

> refusing relations in which people experiencing poverty are seen as objects of knowledge to be 'grasped' by those with power and privilege, whether through reading statistics and written evidence or through hearing testimonies face-to-face.
>
> (Radford, 2022: 195)

To exhibit their plight for the contemplation of an academic audience or public at large feels wrong. The only volunteer I would have for such an interview would be the wealthy 'Tim Nice-but-Dim', a fictional, wealthy dim-witted character from a television comedy.

This is why my third example, although coming from someone with a disadvantaged background (the greatest pool of BSC), represents both the BSC and its complete opposite; not a 'top set citizen' but the phoenix-like resilience and creativity required to survive and rise beyond bottom set segregation. Jay Blades, the creator of the BBC television programme *The repair shop*, admits in his biography to have been a vulnerable youth. The difference between him and Farage or Trump is that Jay was able to turn his life around and leave his Bottom-Set ways behind, most probably out of maturity and an unrecognized, sheer natural intelligence.

In using Farage and Trump as examples of current BSC, I am certain that nothing I can say could dent their self-esteem or public image. However, this does not mean that I can laugh at them or present them as bad persons necessarily. Just imagine what they might have been, had they been encouraged to develop epistemic virtue from childhood. Wealthier children may not be suffering a social injustice, but they may be equally vulnerable to epistemic ones taking place within school. We ignore their plight to society's detriment too. Feelings of shame and humiliation are universal, what we do about them on the other hand, is in part shaped by the community surrounding us. 'It never did me any harm' speaks to cases where injustices on children have been deeply felt by them and support or ameliorating actions from adults mostly absent. Such children grow up to believe that their lot reflects 'just the way of the world', and they may support the same injustices on other people's children, who in turn learn the meaning of 'stiff upper lip' all too well.

Finally, I admit that all three of my cases involve men as examples of BS citizenry. I account for this, partly, through the notion of the invisibility of girls in the classroom (Charlton et al., 2007; Gillies, 2016), and generally in society. I have yet to encounter a female voice who publicly declares (or arrogantly demonstrates) to have experienced bottom set relegation on a permanent basis. Tig Notaro, the American stand-up comedian, writer, actor, and radio contributor, famously said on various occasions that she failed three grades at school (8th grade twice) finally dropping out altogether before high school. With her usual deadpan humour she adds, 'The only thing I regret is that I didn't drop out sooner. … It made more sense to me to kind of … drop out and get a job and … live my life' (Notaro,

2012). She acknowledges that her homelife contributed to her quirkiness, but it shows us how ill-prepared many schools are when it comes to accommodating children whose talents are neither academic nor sporty. Often, being placed in 'low ability' groups is only indicative of schools not having an alternative or at least wider conception of the diverse repertoire of human ability/intelligence. In a Netflix documentary, the footballer David Beckham admits his perceived 'low intellectual ability' status to the reporter at the time, by saying to him, 'I'm not very intelligent'. He now probably understands that what he should have said was simply that he was 'not particularly academic'. We understand that there are differences in children's academic abilities. That is not under question here. The issue arises only when we segregate children within class or within school on that account. To sentence a child 'to be exposed before your peers', as Pink Floyd (1979b) once said, is no trifling matter.

Such segregation is what can make a young person learn to present themselves as 'not intelligent' to others (and worst, to themselves). Beckham had the advantage of excelling at football ... but he is an exception.

On exemplars of epistemic revolt

Feeling humiliated by others because of a perceived inferior intellectual ability can impact both moral and intellectual virtues, and leave individuals to reinvent themselves as best they can. Assuming that we are all born as potentially good persons, willing and capable of embracing virtue given the opportunity, to suffer epistemic injustice can impact us deeply,

> it can cramp self-development, so that a person may be, quite literally, prevented from becoming who they are.
> (Fricker, 2007: 5)

Trump and Farage, just like the homeless, I believe, were prevented from becoming who they could have been; persons able to flourish in positive ways. However, whereas the homeless' primary injustices are of a social nature, for Trump and Farage the injustice is epistemic; concerning mainly their nurtured relation to notions of truth and knowledge. Thus, they can be Conspiracy Theorists (Cassam, 2019) par excellence. They have, for instance, a divergent understanding (I say it with generosity) of such concepts as truth and honesty, concepts that used to feature high among the expected virtues of politicians, but less so now (Runciman, 2018). Still, we are reminded of the necessary nuances required to understand honesty as a virtue,

> The honest person recognises "That would be a lie" as a strong (though perhaps not overriding) reason for not making certain statements in certain circumstances, and gives due, but not overriding, weight to "That would be the truth" as a reason for making them.
>
> (Hursthouse and Pettigrove, 2023: 4)

Based on virtue theory of direct reference, Zagzebski (2017) developed what she called an Exemplarist Moral Theory. The theory poses that we understand, for instance, what 'goodness' or 'honesty' is, through the experience of having encountered admirable persons exemplifying such virtues, rather than through a theoretical evaluation of the virtues themselves; personal encounter being 'more reliable than any theoretical mechanism by which we might try to justify them' (Clark, 2019: 276). Zagzebski notes,

> I want to make the foundation of my theory something that most of us trust—the people we admire upon reflection. The structure is foundationalist, but instead of starting with a concept, the theory begins with exemplars of moral goodness identified directly by the emotion of admiration.
>
> (Zagzebski, 2017: 10)

It may seem misguided to offer Trump or Farage as exemplars of virtues. But the reasons why we admire people are not necessarily virtuous in themselves nor does it mean that those we admire are virtuous in all respects (Cassam, 2019). People can be both admirable and immoral (Archer and Matheson, 2021). We may admire courage in some people or circumstances but not in others. Do we, for instance, admire honesty regardless of tactfulness and consequences?

Some of the examples I offer are necessarily fictional while others are real public figures. For instance, an example of cultural inaccuracy for me was to see that Ron Weasley (somewhat inept character) sat right next to Hermione Granger (a swat) in class, throughout their whole school life. No grouping by ability in Harry Potter ... what else is a fantasy?

It was their friendship and not a school's meritocratic view of maximizing intellectual ability that was to be instrumental to their success as fictional characters. Rightly so. Ron would often complain about Hermione's revision timetables for him and Harry, but all three passed their end-of-year exams. Although both Ron and Harry were aware of Hermione's high academic intellect (and arrogant manners), they were never physically placed in opposition to it (and hence her). It would be admirable if all schools in Britain emulated that aspect of Harry Potter.

Tim Nice-but-Dim is another fictional character brought to life by comedian Harry Enfield in the 1990s. Tim provides an example of the scorn that those deem to be 'low ability' often receive. Although Tim himself is an absurd extreme example, the scorn he receives is not. In one of the sketches, after being repeatedly insulted by a 'clever man' working in a book shop, Tim declares him to be a '*Bloody nice bloke ... for a swat anyway*'. Tim is never much faced by circumstances, and even remembers with fondness a scriptures master as a '*Bloody good bloke. He used to beat me every day—I'm very grateful to him for that of course. It made me the man I am now*'. Impatient and irritated, the 'clever man' ultimately exclaims, '*Get out of my shop. You, pathetic, inbred individual*'. At one point, in a postmodernist fashion (Gogglebox-like), Enfield inserts an aside of two working-class men who, having watched (like us) the sketch and what transpired between Tim and other 'clever actors', cannot understand why such a state of affairs would be amusement to anyone. They exclaim, '*What the bloody hell is all that about! It's just a thick bloke. What's the point of that! I can't believe it*'. Like some of Tolstoy's short stories, the only actors that get hot under the collar are the supposedly 'clever men', whether working or middle class. It is interesting to observe though, that it is the working-class men who are made to object to the amusement value of the sketch. They seem, in a crude way, to show either greater compassion for Tim's plight and discard the humiliation observed by us (but unfelt by Tim), or, they believe that there is no amusement value in portraying a 'dim' person talking, who is unaware of the humiliating (and amusing) element of the exchange. But the latter would turn them into 'partly dim' as well. In this sense their intervention is contradictory, for although Tim may be 'dim', the other 'clever actors' are placed as definitely dull by contrast (a bookshop assistant and an art critic).

But what about us, the 'real' viewers? Where do *we* see the amusement? Enfield's characters are known for being acutely stereotypical and are often used as reference material (Benedictus, 2015). In a strange way, just like the working-class men we are also part of the sketch, but unlike them, we don't realize. We believe ourselves above it, or that such a situation is not really about us. The sketch reassures us. Whether we are middle or working class, we know one thing for certain: we are not like Tim. We know when we are being humiliated. The fact that he is wealthy makes it safe to laugh at him when we see him treated derogatorily by others; his humiliation is our amusement, particularly because it goes over his head. Thus, the working-class men are right in unexpected ways; there is no amusement value without *us* in on it. Rather than a comedy, the whole thing is a tragedy. A very British tragedy, which I am perpetuating here, not because Tim is cushioned by wealth, but because he, as a person, is fictional and serves a good point. The likes of Farage or Trump on the other hand, ought not to be laughed at for they are real persons. With every laugh from us their contempt for us increases. After all, they've been used to others' intellectual scorn since childhood. And although we cannot help them (too late for that), we cannot look away either. They mean business.

In this respect, both Trump and Farage are examples of BSCs as an abstraction. That is to say, they may never have been in actual 'bottom sets' or 'low tracks' in the ordinary classroom, but this is because they were never in an ordinary classroom as such. They had no ordinary childhoods. Both received private education which, as I have said, somewhat cushions the blow of being 'not the intellectual sort'. And yet, in their biographies and public life, one can appreciate the 'looking away', the 'cold shoulder' towards the intellectual elite that publicly humiliates them—to their indifference, for they have had to become well-groomed ducks in that respect. Being in a private school helped Farage to reach college with mediocre results (Crick, 2022) and money helped Trump to get a Bachelor of Science degree, the validity of which many have questioned. This does not stop them from being exemplars of BSCs because I believe that had they been nurtured into epistemic virtue in their schooling years, rather than ridiculed for being oddities in an intellectually competitive system, they may have turned out to be more empathic if not compassionate individuals.

If education is meant to encourage intellectual virtues, then it ought to shape individuals who are, 'deeply and fundamentally motivated by epistemic ends like knowledge and understanding' (Baehr, 2011: 209), which is clearly not Farage's or Trump's case. Their education denied

118 *'It never did me any harm'*

them this, for I do not believe that as children they had such anti-intellectual agendas. But if we separate the intellectual from the moral, what sort of nurturing virtue was available to them in school or learning context? After all, both of them flourished as persons in the world of business and public life, but 'flourishing' in itself has no particular moral propensity,

> We sometimes make judgments to the effect that "So-and-so may be an excellent athlete or musician or chef, but he's a complete jerk," where the latter, I am suggesting, is at least sometimes equivalent to "he's morally rotten." There is little reason to doubt that while the subjects of such judgments are defective from a moral standpoint, their athletic or artistic abilities still aim at and contribute to some aspect of their flourishing as human beings. While they may not be flourishing on the whole, and are not flourishing morally, presumably they still exhibit a distinctively human variety of excellence or enjoy a distinctively human kind of well-being. If so, then we cannot think of moral virtues merely as personal qualities aimed at human flourishing.
>
> (Baehr, 2011: 212)

Bearing this in mind, let us explore the 'distinctively human variety of excellence and well-being' that allowed Farage and Trump to flourish.

A stiff upper lip: an example from a private UK school

Greenhayes School for Boys, Eden Park Preparatory School, and Dulwich College in London, have together helped produce one of their most celebrated (and infamous) contemporary citizens: Nigel Farage.

Farage had made an impact (not academic) on those private schools even then. Fairlamb, one of his teachers remembers having said to him, 'Nigel, I have a feeling that you will go far in life. But whether in fame or infamy, I don't really know'. Fairlamb adds that Farage looked back at him and replied, 'Sir, as long as it's far I don't care which' (Crick, 2022: 36). Farage's biographies, either in his own words or through others' research, are full of such quoted 'banter'; off-the-cuff, often offensive, or entertaining remarks that made some laugh and others squirm.

As Wikipedia describes him, Farage is 'a British broadcaster and former politician', but in the United Kingdom his claim to fame—or

'It never did me any harm' 119

infamy, is that he led Great Britain out of the European Union, in a Pied Piper of Hamelin-like fashion, in what became known as Brexit. The tactics he used were immigration and the element of 'Britishness'. Both concepts allow notions of 'them and us' to flourish and to be exploited, and require little mental effort to enact.

Even in his formative years, Farage was against everyone in the establishment. The fact that he was not the academic sort, together with his admiration for the likes of Enoch Powell (the British politician who fervently opposed the anti-discrimination legislation laws), his antisemitic and fascist comments, and his delight in sharing the same initials as the National Front, did not stop the Headmaster at Dulwich College from turning him into a prefect.

Farage was in most ways, an 'odd person' judged by the recollections from staff and students (Crick, 2022). That Farage was deeply affected by events in his early childhood that may have had nothing to do with academic ability cannot be denied. By the time he got to Dulwich College his personality seems to have been set in many ways. However, the competitive nature of the school in terms of academic or sporty performance did not help contribute a sense of epistemic virtue in Farage. Quite the opposite. The decision to make him a prefect, despite a very strong case made against it, may have convinced him that his path was praiseworthy.
Like Tim, he remembers the words from his career's master with fondness,

> He must have spotted that I was quite ballsy, probably good on a platform, unafraid of the limelight, a bit noisy and good at selling things. All of those traits were identified, nurtured and promoted at Dulwich College. ... I was told by [him] that I should aim for a job as an auctioneer.
>
> (Farage, 2015)

I am not sure if Farage was aware of the deprecatory nature of the comment. After all, most students sitting their Advanced Level at 18, are not doing so in the hope of working as an auctioneer. Instead of going into university, Farage became a commodities trader. He was certainly good at selling things, and the first item he must have sold was a different narrative of himself, to himself. Farage was turned into an excellent storyteller by circumstances, including school. His traits allowed him, by age 35, to be elected to the European Parliament, and in 2018, he auctioned Britain's future in the EU to the most ardent buyers; the disenfranchised. The contempt in which the establishment and the intellectual elites held Farage was well-known by him and the media,

> All these attacks, Farage told the London crowd, just show how rattled the establishment are, how much they want to deny you, the people, the Brexit you voted for.
> This is [Farage's] modus operandi—borrowed, it has to be said, straight from Donald Trump. If you pose as an outsider, then every scandalous revelation can be presented as a desperate attack by the elite, bent on stifling your voice—and, through you, the voice of the people.
>
> (Freedland, 2019)

Except that Farage seemed to be an outsider since his childhood. Whatever he has been part of, he rallies against. And yet, no one is born with a resentment towards the establishment. He seems never to have been part, as a child or adult, of a supportive, collaborative (as opposed to competitive and hierarchical) community. It is no wonder that his unauthorized biography is called, From Party to Party. His statements have been false and misleading at the best of times, and he is clearly intelligent enough to entwine them with people's daily concerns. He may not have been the academic sort at school, but in the academic contempt he did receive, his contrary attitude only grew stronger. Whatever was nurtured in him wherever he went, epistemic virtue was not part of it.

As for his followers, many needed little encouragement to show their own contempt for the establishment that belittled them. Tim Nice-but-Dim would have voted for Farage. The workmen watching the sketch may have voted for him too. Only the so called 'clever men' in the sketch and the 'clever' viewers at home probably didn't. The tabloids understood the intellectual elites' contempt for Farage all too well, when the day after the Brexit referendum they printed, impersonating the intellectual elites,

> You stupid people. You got it wrong again. You were supposed to vote for candidates determined to stop Brexit, or at least stay at home and leave Britain's future to the experts.

'It never did me any harm' 121

> What the hell did you think you were doing voting for that dreadful fascist Farage person and his raggle-taggle gang of Trumpist racists, Russian stooges and rabid Little Englanders?
>
> (The Mail online, 2019)

Five years later, a study claimed that most of the people who voted for Brexit were more likely to be of 'lower cognitive ability' (Dawson and Baker, 2023). Still, at the time Farage celebrated the referendum result by reminding the nation all they had fought for (and won), in a speech that makes him appear as the rescuer of all virtues,

> We have fought against big politics, we have fought against lies, corruption and deceit, ... And we will have done it without having to fight, without a single bullet being fired. We'd have done it by damned hard work on the ground. ... but what we've proved is the British are too big to bully, thank goodness.
>
> (Farage, 2015)

'Damned hard work on the ground' is exactly what enabled him to get a victory, but not *his* hard work. It is an education system of segregation, among other social injustices, that did the hard work on the ground. An educational system that encouraged many people not to engage with critical reflection or notions of honesty and truth in knowledge; a system that made people find their virtues elsewhere. When wealthy children encounter such treatment they can become empowered bottom set citizens.

Further evidence of Farage's disdain for the intellectual and political elites can be appreciated in the speech he gave to the members of the European Parliament,

> I know that virtually none of you have ever done a proper job in your lives, or worked in business, or worked in trade, or indeed ever created a job.
>
> (Guardian News, 2016)

Despite the booing from the MEPs, Farage stood triumphant. He had flourished against all the odds set by 'the establishment'. His special kind of well-being appears to be entirely of his own making. But this is not quite so. The values that our education system imparted did not help him or other children find any joy or self-worth in the school experience pertaining to knowledge and understanding. We do not see, as members of the establishment Farage claims to abhor, that we helped create the likes of him. Nothing, therefore, has been altered in our education system since. I imagine it is because 'as an empire' Britain also enjoys a warped sense of flourishing, a 'distinctively human variety of excellence and well-being' that financially benefits those in power.

'You know, I'm, like, a smart person' (an American example)

These were Donald Trump's words for Fox News in 2016. Trump, considering himself to be already a smart person, could not see the point of having Intelligence Briefings every morning. Trump's statements about his mental ability, physical prowess, personality, etc., range between the assertive to the extravagant and the absurd. A fraction of such statements include:

> I've been known as being a very smart guy for a long time.
> I have a very good brain and I've said a lot of things.
> I'm intelligent. Some people would say I'm very, very, very intelligent.
> And then people say oh, is he a smart person? I'm smarter than all of them put together, but they can't admit it.
> My IQ is one of the highest—and you all know it! Please don't feel so stupid or insecure; it's not your fault.
> My two greatest assets have been mental stability and being, like, really smart … . I went from VERY successful businessman, to top T.V. Star, to President of the United States (on my first try). I think that would qualify as not smart, but genius … . and a very stable genius at that!
>
> (in Stewart, 2018)

If Trump has learned anything in his life, it is that intelligence is a sort of decision rather than a trait; a *stance* that the establishment favours. As such, it is not only worth claiming to possess it, but such claims are essential towards credibility and dominance over others. Thus, we can be intelligent by the mere act of saying so. In a televised Newspress in South Carolina (2015), Trump referred to politicians' efforts to bring peace to Syria as 'stupid' rather than 'incompetent' because, as he said,

'It never did me any harm' 123

I went to an Ivy League school. I'm very highly educated. I know words. I have the best words. But there's no better word than stupid, right? There is none.

It is difficult to quote Trump's words without feeling we are in some way laughing at him; exposing his intellectual naivety and egotistical prowess, something I did not wish to do. To laugh is only to betray the contempt we hold him in, and those like him. It exposes *us* as members of an arrogant, intolerant, and oppressive intellectual elite. Just like with the workmen from the comedy sketch earlier who did not see the point of an audience laughing at Tim Nice-but-Dim, our laugh betrays our sense of superiority; our misguided belief that our laugh has the power—through the ensued potential humiliation—to make him rethink his position/words; to force him to reflection. But we already lost the privilege to help educate his mind to these ends. Our laugh only makes him more resolute.

The saddest element in all of Trump's assertions (apart from actual harm) is that he believes them to be true, or at least to suffice. According to his unauthorized biography, written by his niece, psychologist Mary L. Trump, Trump's early upbringing environment was a place of humiliation and overbearing expectations for the eldest son (Fred) and harsh indifference towards the rest, who were allowed to indulge the quickest route to superiority and achievement. Lying and stepping over others became Trump's best survival tool. This is how he was allowed to flourish.

When such an upbringing is empowered by a life of financial privilege, changing the narrative of one's life becomes all too easy. The education he received outside his home did not help. Trump's behaviour at primary school had become so defiant that he was sent to what was known to most in the family as a 'reform school',

> Nobody sent their sons to NYMA [a military boarding school] for a better education, and Donald understood it rightly as a punishment.
> (Mary Trump, 2020: 50)

When little weight is placed on the cultivation of virtues at home, school becomes all the more important. Unable to not only 'be the best' academically but seeing that he in fact struggled in this respect; that his intellectual faculties were not under his control must have been unbearable. Effort, made no difference. He threatened, through a former aid, to sue the college he had attended if they ever made his grades or SAT scores public. And yet, he questioned Obama's suitability for presidency,

> "I heard he was a terrible student, terrible" Trump declared in 2011. "How does a bad student go to Colombia and then to Harvard? ... Let him show his records."
>
> (Sandel, 2020: 81)

As a financially empowered BSC, in the eyes of other, disempowered and epistemically vulnerable BSCs, Trump is intelligent by merely claiming to be so. No evidence is needed besides the assertion, for the assertion is the thing itself. On winning Nevada he proclaimed,

> We won the evangelicals, we won with young, we won with old, we won with highly educated—we won with poorly educated. I *love* the poorly educated [gesturing with arms]. We're the smartest people we're the most loyal people.
>
> (Trump, 2016)

When Trump mentions 'the highly educated' he doesn't get any cheers, and, realizing that a different approach was needed, he not only adds 'the poorly educated' but claims to love them, getting cheers from the crowd. The crowd sees him as one of them in terms of Trump's own contempt for the establishment that belittles him. His virtue, in their eyes, is being who he is. Despite evidence of lying and of misogynist remarks and actions, Trump is still admired by his followers, partly because they either do not believe the evidence which they see as 'fake news' (Polletta and Callahan, 2017) or simply because such evidence does not trump the admirable traits they see in him. When Archer and Matheson ponder how an immoral person can be admirable, 'and whether immorality can ever affect a person's admirability' (Archer and Matheson, 2021: 23), some may need go no further than to offer Donald Trump as an exemplar.

When a reporter interviewed some of Trump's followers at a rally in Iowa, and confronted them with 'verified facts', it becomes clear that Trump's admirability rests on emotional rather than rational aspects,

> "I want the economy back to the way it was. I thought he did a good job when he was in there." [when evidence is presented to the

contrary] "Yeah, that's their opinion. They're not the ones that have to worry about going to the gas pump and pumping gas that's almost five bucks a gallon. When Trump was in there it was a dollar something."
"Our country was at its highest point when he was president. We need to get back to what it used to be, because I think our country was a lot happier and less divided when he was president." [when confronted with evidence to the contrary] "Yeah, he says some stupid stuff—the tweets and everything—but that doesn't bother me because ultimately he's an honest, truthful person. I like his personality. I like that he's a businessman."

(Smith, *The Guardian*, 2023)

In 'What Does Morality Have to Do with It?' Brisbane (2023) explores for instance, why evangelical communities in US admire Trump with such fervour. She makes reference to the type of morality that 'binds and blinds'. Evangelical voters saw Trump as,

a warrior for their evangelical Christianity's conservative efforts to bring God back into the political sphere and a protector of their patriotic sensibilities.

(Brisbane, 2023: 16)

There is no 'ability grouping' when it comes to faith or patriotism, and seen in this light, we might understand why they trump rational scrutiny, which requires intellectual engagement with verified sources. In their eyes, it is God and not other people (nor education nor money), who makes us feel truly equal, special even, and worthy; similarly, patriotism can put us on an equal footing with the most able or richest of persons. Brisbane, through her many interviews, was able to show that it is the God-like devotion for Trump that many voters displayed, which stops them from criticizing elements that destabilize their own identities.

How someone can be religious while at the same time critical and reflective of their own position and knowledge base, is not something Brisbane's participants may have encountered in their formative years. After all, religion can also be a refuge from the overbearing contempt of others. Why would we open the door to having others show us how wrong we have been all our lives, particularly when, with contempt, they offer us no viable alternatives. Thus, faith can appear to give us the certainty of righteousness in our moral attitudes to the world, 'while reasoning is more of an afterthought' (ibid.).

For the evangelical community, the Bible appears to lend the necessary dogma needed to blindly admire Trump. The values mostly attributed to him by the participants were 'honesty' and 'integrity', but even when these were shown to be lacking in Trump, supporters countered it with, 'no one is perfect'. Passion and resentment override all reason. As Victor Hugo observed,

> Whoever cherishes in his soul a secret revolt against any deed whatever on the part of the state, of life or of fate, is ripe for riot, and, as soon as it makes its appearance, he begins to quiver, and to feel himself borne away with the whirlwind.
>
> *Les Misérables* (1832)

Trump gives his followers the quickest and most dramatic ticket to power; he gives them what the establishment never did: the idea of being embraced, which can be empowering experiences when you have suffered nothing but contempt from,

a the intellectually meritocratic elites who made you believe that your educational failures were your own fault for not putting in the required effort, or simply for possessing 'inferior' academic abilities, which can lead you to embrace what can embrace you back; faith over science (i.e. creationism, Flat Earth Society, etc.), and,

b from a post-imperial, meritocratic system that supports this, arguing that one's condition in life is simply of one's own making.

For the latter, at least, Trump's followers may feel empowered to do one thing: to vote for him is to vote for what is left of me. But voting, as Dewey reminds us, is the easy part, for democracy is tested in its processes not in the voting. Ability grouping is a counterproductive instance of such processes, for it pushes children into reactive rather than reflective attitudes; a kind of epistemic darkness. Attempting to rescue the BSC from the stance of epistemic privilege, is ineffective, particularly when there is no trust.

'Repairing my life' (an example of UK resilience)

The third case is the briefest of them all. It represents what it means to have survived BS citizenry and to have left it behind as an adult.

Unlike Farage or Trump, Jay Blades as he is now, is *not* an example of a BSC—he just used to be one.

Coming from a disadvantaged background and against all the odds, Jay was able to, as he put it, repair his life, becoming famous—while still unable to read or write—for his BBC show *The repair shop*. Undiagnosed dyslexia saw him relegated to the 'low ability' groups in primary/elementary years, and to the bottom set classes in secondary school, where he was, as he says, 'written-off'. He recollects his days in the 'lower' stream,

> My school split each year into three streams the Ps, the Ms and the L's. I still don't know what they stood for, but we used to call them the Perfects, the Mediums and the Learners—or probably it should have been the *Losers* ... The L lessons were licensed anarchy. I'd walk into the class to find yelling and missiles flying about everywhere. Most days the teacher might as well not have been there. There were a lot of very, very naughty kids in the Ls. I quickly became one of them. ... I didn't learn a single thing and I didn't expect to. In the Ls we all knew we weren't going to get academic qualifications or go off to university. We didn't care.
> (Blades, 2021: 35)

Coping with racism and the injustices and indifferences he experienced in school, meant learning to fight back, and fight first. It meant looking for an alternative story; a narrative of success,

> some days I'd get a bad beating. But soon I was winning a lot more fights than I was losing. I earned myself a reputation—and the sad thing was. *I got to love fighting.* You always love what you are good at.
> (ibid.: 33)

Jay Blades left school with no qualifications. Like Farage, he recalls his careers teacher,

> the guy just stared at me from behind his desk and laughed. 'Well, you're going to amount to nothing, Blades!' He smirked. 'It's not even worth talking to you'. ... We L-stream kids didn't sit many exams and the handful that I did were totally futile.
> (ibid.: 50)

As a young adult Jay went to prison for 3 years and was homeless for another 3, which may have proved his teacher right in the eyes of some. But at age 30, he experienced the necessity of change,

> My life felt like a mess; a mistake; a dead-end. *This isn't where I want to be. This isn't the person I want to be.*
>
> (ibid.: 132)

But perhaps, he had always had the seedling for the kind of person he wanted to be, it was just that school encouraged him *not* to nurture his moral and intellectual virtues.

In ways that are not clear, Jay somehow managed to get accepted in a university course. He made his own way into epistemic virtue; wanting to understand and know why things are the way they are; what can be done to make things better for oneself and for others. He got a 2:1 in Criminology and Philosophy. You can learn about his incredible journey in his books, 'Making It: How Love, Kindness and Community Helped Me Repair My Life' and 'Life Lessons: Wisdom and Wit from Life's Ups and Downs'.

I need only leave you with the kind of insights he already had as a young boy, with his best friend, Iqbal,

> One day, I was walking down a corridor at school. I saw Iqbal with his back to me. He had his head down and was fiddling with something.
> 'Hey Iqbal! You OK?' I asked him.
> He turned around. I saw the tearstains on his face. 'Jay, I can't fix them,' he said.
> 'Fix what?'
> Iqbal held his glasses out to me. They were only NHS specs and the bullies had smashed them so many times that there was more Sellotape on them than there was glass or frame. And now there was no room for any more.
> 'I can't fix them this time,' he said.
> It was heartbreaking. I knew Iqbal's family were poor, like mine, and they couldn't afford to buy him new specs. Even now, forty years on, I choke up at the memory of that poor, sweet kid holding out his ruined glasses. He looked so forlorn—so unhappy.
> I looked at Iqbal and something in me snapped ...
>
> (ibid.: 32)

This exchange, which took place when Jay was but 12 years old, shows us the kind of virtues he was already prone to, but which only his friends, community, and adult self were able to see and value. Damaging school (and life) experiences, when left unexamined, can lead to denial (Renton, 2017), making us say things like, 'It never did me any harm'. This is evident in the self-satisfaction that comes through in Farage and Trump, my BSC exemplars. They, like Jay, were denied the opportunity to develop epistemic virtue in their formative years. Jay, however, unlike them, was surrounded by a different community. The challenges he faced pushed him to the brink of experience, forcing him to examine his life. School was one of the aspects in his formative years that prevented him from becoming the person he really was meant to be.

Schools, please stop. 'I have become comfortably numb'

I close this book with an anthem. The phrase, 'comfortably numb' comes from the Pink Floyd album, The Wall (1979a), and serves here a triple purpose. First, The Wall has already highlighted issues of power abuse in schools in terms of corporal punishment and overt humiliation. Epistemic injustice on the other hand, is invisible to the eyes. We only see its outcome: epistemic revolt; which is a warped relationship with notions of truth, knowledge and one's identity, and which is expressed through epistemic vices (e.g. constant lying, cruelty, relativizing virtues, indifference/numbness, etc.).

Second, it exemplifies the state of accustomed powerlessness that comes from being labelled as 'low ability', whatever the euphemism employed. Children have no choice but to accept adults' decisions to gain their approval or until something snaps, for a sense of worth must be obtained somehow. But 'how does "morality" deal with the many reasons for behaving badly that lie in the desire to be loved?' (Williams and Wood, 2014: 246). That is, how do *we* deal with this question in the school context? When children realize that adult approval is futile (for no amount of effort is getting me out of the 'lower ability' group), their desire to be loved and accepted can only be achieved by turning their back on academic knowledge; children's need for approval and safety can only be met by each other, which is a dangerous (a wild) place to be.

Third, Roger Waters has been criticized for being rather misogynistic in his approach to despair, and yet, it is in fact our boys that are the most *visibly* impacted by the practice of ability grouping (Love, 2014; Raey, 2017; Archer et al., 2018). Boys' need for some kind of status among their peers (Boor-Klip et al., 2017), however naïve a need, is highly challenged by ability grouping practices. For girls, the practice may well thicken the invisibility veil they already have. But invisibility does not do away with issues.

Ultimately, being placed in 'low ability' groups, at whatever end of the economic or intelligence spectrum, and in whatever context, is a recipe for social disaster in any democracy. It does not mean that some children are not intelligent, far from it, it means only that their intelligence, or whatever academic ability they have, is not recognized or nurtured towards epistemic virtue. It goes unnoticed; left to flourish as the child sees best. It is little wonder that such a citizen can only vote for what appears to relate to his own, immediate concerns. Little wonder that he or she can be taken advantage of by more powerful BSCs. Segregating children by ability benefits no one.

> As Sandel (2020) acknowledges on the last page of the book: '[Democracy] require that citizens from different walks of life encounter one another in common spaces and public places' (p. 227). Segregation, then, may be the most formidable obstacle to common life and the common good.
>
> (Mijs, 2022: 177)

The academic world may be barking up the wrong tree when they think that only further, more robust evidence (quantitative, empirical, longitudinal, etc.) can make governments stop ability grouping practices from the top. Governments are listening to a different, self-serving tune of their own, which involves meritocracy's allegiance to the riches of empire. Studies will not change practices that are borne and nested in unacknowledged, long-held values and received beliefs. First, many academics would need to relinquish any awards bestowed on them by the Empire (OBE, MBE) to have any credibility. Their hard work must, of course, be celebrated, but not on behalf of the empire, which would undermine any cause.

Schools, please stop.

I am not saying that ability grouping practices are solely responsible for issues of inequality in education. I am only saying that having the power to eliminate the practice and *not* make things worse, is within teachers', schools' and education systems' power, and yet, no one acts. Why don't they act? I am saying that, having the opportunity to encourage epistemic virtue in all students, and particularly in the most vulnerable, they make a point of encouraging such virtues only in the few; I argue that schools' silent belief in imperial values around hierarchies and competition makes them embrace unjust meritocratic practices and disregard or belittle the mounting evidence against it and against ability grouping. I am saying that children's rights, i.e. Article 29.1.a, 'the education of the child shall be directed to the development of the child's personality, talents and mental and physical abilities to their fullest potential' ought not to be done for the few at the expense of most others. Unless of course, education systems, like Farage, Trump or any empire, also practice a perverse and distinctively human variety of excellence and flourishing.

Children, like Jay, deserve more than a fleeting glimpse of their potential virtues.

Let us not encourage any more bottom set citizens, disengaged from a search for true democratic processes, for it will ultimately hurt us all.

> When I was a child, I had a flitting glimpse
> Out of the corner of my eye
> I turned to look, but it was gone
> I cannot put my finger on it, now
> The child has grown, the dream is gone
> I, have become, comfortably numb.
>
> (Pink Floyd, 1979a)

References

Archer, L., Francis, B., Miller, S., Taylor, B., Tereshchenko, A., Mazenod, A., Pepper, D., & Travers, M.-C. (2018). The symbolic violence of setting: A Bourdieusian analysis of mixed methods data on secondary students' views about setting. *British Educational Research Journal, 44*(1), 119–140. https://doi.org/10.1002/berj.3321

Baehr, J. S. (2011). *The inquiring mind: On intellectual virtues and virtue epistemology.* University Press.

Benedictus, L. (2015). The enduring social shorthand of Harry Enfield characters. *The Guardian.* www.theguardian.com/tv-and-radio/shortcuts/2015/jul/27/enduring-social-shorthand-harry-enfield-characters

Blades, J. (2021). *Making it: How love, kindness and community helped me repair my life (main market edition).* Bluebird.

Boor-Klip, H. J., Segers, E., Hendrickx, M. M. H. G., & Cillessen, A. H. N. (2017). The moderating role of classroom descriptive norms in the association of student behavior with social preference and popularity. *The Journal of Early Adolescence, 37*(3), 387–413. https://doi.org/10.1177/0272431615609158

Brisbane, G. J. (2023). What does morality have to do with it? What Haidt and moral foundation theory reveals about white evangelical Christian women who advocate for politician Donald J. Trump. *Howard Journal of Communications, 34*(5), 1–19. https://doi.org/10.1080/10646175.2023.2212624

Cassam, Q. (2019). *Conspiracy theories.* Polity Press.

Charlton, E., Mills, M., Martino, W., & Beckett, L. (2007). Sacrificial girls: A case study of the impact of streaming and setting on gender reform. *British Educational Research Journal, 33*(4), 459–478.

Clark, P. (2019). Exemplarist Moral Theory by Linda Trinkaus Zagzebski (review). *Nova et Vetera, 17*(1), 275–284.

Craven, K., Sapra, S., Harmon, J., & Hyde, M. (2022). "I'm No Criminal, I'm Just Homeless": The Greensboro Homeless Union's efforts to address the criminalization of homelessness. *Journal of Community Psychology, 50*(4), 1875–1892.

Crick, M. (2022). *One party after another: The disruptive life of Nigel Farage.* Simon & Schuster.

D'Ath, P. J., Keywood, L. J., Styles, E. C., & Wilson, C. M. (2016). East London's homeless: A retrospective review of an eye clinic for homeless people. *BMC Health Services Research, 16*(54), 54–54.

Dawson, C., & Baker, P. L. (2023). Cognitive ability and voting behaviour in the 2016 UK referendum on European Union membership. *PLOS ONE, 18*(11), e0289312.

Farage, N. (2015). Nigel Farage: My public school had a real social mix, but now only the mega-rich can afford the fees. *The Telegraph.* www.telegraph.co.uk/news/politics/nigel-farage/11467039/Nigel-Farage-My-public-school-had-a-real-social-mix-but-now-only-the-mega-rich-can-afford-the-fees.html

Freedland, J. (2019, May 22). Why is Nigel Farage immune to scandals that would destroy his rivals? *The Guardian.* www.theguardian.com/commentisfree/2019/may/22/nigel-farage-scandals-rivals-brexit-party-european-elections

Fricker, M. (2007). Epistemic injustice: Power and the ethics of knowing. In *Epistemic injustice.* Oxford University Press.

Gillies, V. (2016). Damaged boys, needy girls. In Gillies, V. (Ed.), *Pushed to the edge* (1st ed., pp. 77–100). Bristol University Press. https://doi.org/10.2307/j.ctt1t897th.7

'It never did me any harm' 133

Guardian News (Director). (2016, June 28). *Nigel Farage to MEPs: 'most of you have never done a proper job'*. www.youtube.com/watch?v=40ul e97jkRA

Hugo, V. (1832). *Les Misérables*, Five Volumes, Complete by Victor Hugo. www.gutenberg.org/files/135/135-h/135-h.htm#link2HCH0266

Hursthouse, R., & Pettigrove, G. (2023). Virtue ethics. In E. N. Zalta & U. Nodelman (Eds.), *The Stanford encyclopedia of philosophy* (Fall 2023). Metaphysics Research Lab, Stanford University. https://plato.stanford.edu/archives/fall2023/entries/ethics-virtue/

Kyprianides, A., Stott, C., & Bradford, B. (2021). 'Playing the game': Power, authority and procedural justice in interactions between police and homeless people in London. *British Journal of Criminology, 61*(3), 670–689. https://doi.org/10.1093/bjc/azaa086

Littlejohn, R. (2019, May 27). You stupid people. You got it wrong again. *Mail Online*. www.dailymail.co.uk/debate/article-7076141/RICHARD-LITTLEJOHN-stupid-people-got-wrong-again.html

Love, B. L. (2014). "I see Trayvon Martin": What teachers can learn from the tragic death of a young Black male. *The Urban Review, 46*(2), 292–306. https://doi.org/10.1007/s11256-013-0260-7

Mijs, J. J. B. (2022). Merit and ressentiment: How to tackle the tyranny of merit. *Theory and Research in Education, 20*(2), 173–181.

Notaro, T. (Director). (2012). *Tig Notaro: High school dropout*. www.youtube.com/watch?v=i17O1YK2AJA

O'Mahony, B. (1988). *A capital offence: The plight of the young single homeless in London*. Routledge.

Pink Floyd. (1979a). *'Comfortably numb', from album The Wall*. Harvest/EMI and Columbia/CBS Records.

Pink Floyd (1979b). *The Trial, from the album The Wall*. Harvest/EMI and Columbia/CBS Records.

Polletta, F., & Callahan, J. (2017). Deep stories, nostalgia narratives, and fake news: Storytelling in the Trump era. *American Journal of Cultural Sociology, 5*(3), 392–408.

Radford, C. W. (2022). Enacting disruptive encounters. In *Lived experiences and social transformations* (pp. 192–227). Koninklijke Brill. https://doi.org/10.1163/9789004513181_008

Reay, D. (2017). *Miseducation: Inequality, education and the working classes* (1st ed.). Policy Press. https://doi.org/10.2307/j.ctt22p7k7m

Renton, A. (2017). Stiff upper lip: Secrets, crimes and the schooling of a ruling class. Weidenfeld and Nicolson. *History, 102*(352), 712–714. https://doi.org/10.1111/1468-229X.12489

Runciman, D. (2018). *Political hypocrisy: The mask of power, from Hobbes to Orwell and beyond* (Revised Edition – 2nd ed.). Princeton University Press.

Sandel, M. J. (2020). *The tyranny of merit: What's become of the common good?* Allen Lane.

Smith, D. (2023, September 24). 'I like him even better now': Trump's true believers keep the faith. *The Guardian.* www.theguardian.com/us-news/2023/sep/24/donald-trump-supporters-rally-iowa

Stewart, J. M. (2018). Trump's assessment of himself (selected quotes). *HYPERSCAPES.* https://hyperscapes.com/trumps-assessment-selected-quotes/

Trump, Donald, Trump in Nevada: 'I Love the Poorly Educated' CNN. (2016, February 24). www.youtube.com/watch?v=Vpdt7omPoa0

Trump, Mary. L. (2020). Too much and never enough: How my family created the world's most dangerous man. Simon & Schuster. https://uk.bookshop.org/p/books/too-much-and-never-enough-how-my-family-created-the-world-s-most-dangerous-man-ph-d-trump-mary-l/2193526

Williams, B. (2014). *Essays and reviews: 1959–2002* (Course Book). Princeton University Press.

Zagzebski, L. (2017). Why exemplarism? In L. Zagzebski (Ed.), *Exemplarist Moral Theory* (pp. 1–29). Oxford University Press.

Index

Note: Page numbers in *italic* refer to figures.

abstraction: BSC as an 117
academy: intellectual virtues 91
action: connective 103
action: Arendt's definition 65
admiration 115
Alderson, P. 3, 41
Allen, A. 96
American: private education, Trump 122
Anderson, E. 74
Arendt, H. 55, 71
assessment: as means to humiliation 68

Baehr, J. 117, 118
behaviour: management 87
Bernstein, R. 99
Blades, J. 127
Boaler, J. 21
Boys: The History, Bennett's play 56
Brisbane, G. 125
Burris, C. C. 55

Carpenter, J. 100
Cassam, Q. 90
childhood: no democracy in 32; remembering one's 34
Children's Commissioner Report, UK 101
Chilean, revolt 103

citizen: child as emergent 36
citizenry 4, 33, 103
class: social 22
comfortably numb 129
common-sense: Kumashiro 51; a note on 52
community: non- 103
compliance 73
credit: in an action 56

delivery: as lessons' actions 65
democracy: whose? 32
Department for Education 82
Dewey, J. 5, 33, 35, 39, 41
disdain 7, 99, 121
disenfranchised: intellectually 106, 120
Dunne, J. 84

education: private, UK, Farage 118
elites: intellectual 12, 99, 105, 120, 121, 126
empire: meritocracy and its allegiance to 46
empowerment: the idea of 102
Enfield: Harry 116
England: This is, Meadow's film 56
ethical: considerations 111
Eun, B. 81
exemplars 111–17, 129
expectations 23, 24, 36, 86, 123

Index

facts: verified 124
failure: is your own fault 46
Farage, N. 119–21
films 22, 54
flourishing: human 118–22, 131
Francis, B. 19–22, 48
French Revolution 4, 126
Fricker, M. 67, 114
Fundamental British Values 46, 51, 75

Garrity, D. T. 55
gaze: of the empire 51, 72, 84
governmentality 48
grouping: by ability in schools 9
The Guardian 120

Hansen, B. 15
Harry Potter 115
hierarchies: intellectual 53, 102
Hildebrand, D. 32
Horsthemke, K. 107
Hursthouse, R. 115

identification: academic 85
information: as knowledge 64
injustice: epistemic, hermeneutic, structural and testimonial 66–8
intellectual virtues academy *91*, 92
interactions: human 84

Kittay, E. 24
knowing one's place 2, 54
knowledge: suffer 24
knowledge: children and teachers 63
Kosunen, S. 10

Lecercle, J. 88
Legette, K. 70
lion: the tail of 2
Luković, S. 81

The Mail online 121
Martin Chuzzlewitt: Mr Tapley 56
McIntyre, W. 53
media: social 102
Mijs, J. 130
Miller, A. xiii, 41

minorities: ethnic 74
Mlawer, M. 106
modelling 83
most knowledgeable other 6, 78–80

narratives: alternative 86, 92
nation: post-truth 104
natural order 48, 52, 53
neo-liberalism: the habit of empire 50
nonsense: as pedagogical tool 88

Odysseus: the child's journey 59
opinion: relativising knowledge 105
Orchard, J. 39

participation: full 74
patriotism 47, 125
personal experience 4, 25, 63
Pettigrove, G. 115
philosophy 5, 35, 63
Pink Floyd 114
place: you have never been to this *see* knowledge, suffer
power: channels of 72, 85
practices: ability grouping in UK *11*; ability grouping in 4 countries *9*
primary school 1
Pygmalyon: My Fair Lady, Mr Doolittle 56

Radford, C. 112
Raey, D. 98
religion 125
The Repair Shop, 113, 127
research: current on the field 18
resilience: emotional 68
revolt: epistemic 89
rights: of children 40

Sandel, M. 124
school: inclusion example USA *77*, 92; segregation example in UK *65*, 78
secondary school 127
Selwyn, N. 106
Sen, A. 55
Seneviratne, K. 105

Index 137

setting: ability grouping in UK 10
shame: hierarchies of 58
Sokhi-Bulley, B. 48
Stewart, J. 122
strategies: of survival 86
structural responses 72
Suissa, J. 83

the tail of a lion 2, 13
The Two Ronnies 54
theorists: conspiracy 114
Thunberg, G. 38
Towers, E. 20
tracking: ability grouping in USA 15
Trump, Donald 111
Trump, M. 50, 123
Tyson, K. 21

UK: state school example, Blades 126

UK Parliament 33
undeserving, meritocracy's 96

Vaast, E. 104
values: British, imperial 55
vices: epistemic, moral, intellectual 89–91, 129
Victor Hugo, Les Misérables 126
Vygotsky, L. 80, 86

Williams, B. 58, 59
Woods, P. 37

Young, M.: Intro 47, 57, 97, 98
Young, T. 13, 47

Zagzebski, L. 115
Zevenbergen, R. 71, 89
zone of proximal development (ZPD) 80–6, 79

Printed in Great Britain
by Amazon

ba8f29d8-5dbe-4c76-aee5-a92f7912cdf0R01